SOJOURN

SOJOURN

Memories and Reflections

by James V. Isbell

Xulon Press

Xulon Press
555 Winderley Pl, Suite 225
Maitland, FL 32751
407.339.4217
www.xulonpress.com

xulon
PRESS

© 2024 by Jim V. Isbell

All rights reserved solely by the author. The author guarantees all contents are original and do not infringe upon the legal rights of any other person or work. No part of this book may be reproduced in any form without the permission of the author.

Due to the changing nature of the Internet, if there are any web addresses, links, or URLs included in this manuscript, these may have been altered and may no longer be accessible. The views and opinions shared in this book belong solely to the author and do not necessarily reflect those of the publisher. The publisher therefore disclaims responsibility for the views or opinions expressed within the work.

Unless otherwise indicated, Scripture quotations taken from the English Standard Version (ESV). Copyright © 2001 by Crossway, a publishing ministry of Good News Publishers. Used by permission. All rights reserved.

Paperback ISBN-13: 979-8-86850-166-1
eBook ISBN-13: 979-8-86850-167-8

❦ FOREWORD ❦

I have been privileged to walk alongside my friend Jim Isbell as he has recounted his life story and committed it to the typewritten page. And yes, I was one of many who encouraged him to undertake this challenge. He didn't protest, but nor did he have the arrogance of one who felt his story was anything special. Jim would not call himself an accomplished author in any sense of the words, but his narrative captures memories, experiences, observations and reflections with rare transparency, humor, and humility.

And thus, I do believe it is very special. Not so much because of Jim, the man, but because of his Lord and Savior who designed the arc of his life and created him for a special purpose. I know Jim wrote this to bring glory to God; and not to himself. Even that fact makes his story worth reading.

Throughout the past several months, I have reviewed numerous drafts, offered suggestions, and encouraged (sometimes he might say "pushed") him along with his personal narrative. His perspective is well captured in the title… "Sojourn". First, because Jim understands that our earthly life is a temporary stay. We are just passing through enroute to our eternal destiny. Second, because Jim knows we have many choices in the directions we can follow in this life. And Jim traveled more than a few.

But while there may be infinite choices, each has its attendant consequences. Jim reflects on his journey not as an independent agent of fate, but as a grateful recipient of God's grace. In every seemingly insignificant detail, God was there – shaping his trajectory and the arc of his life to make him the man God intended him to be – all the while molding him into a servant, willing to advance the good news of salvation to those who were fortunate to tumble into his orbit.

Jim's life is a story of humble beginnings in a simpler time. Throughout his sojourn, the world has changed dramatically. But God's purpose has not. And I can attest, as Scripture says, that Jim was indeed born "for such a time as this."

As his life unfolded, Jim sometimes rebelled, sometimes practiced the mischief that young boys and young men often fall into. But always present was a genuine sense that God was sovereignly crafting his journey with the precision and purpose of a Master Craftsman.

We are all called to serve in this life – not ourselves as the world would have us believe – but to serve one another. God equipped Jim to serve in myriad roles and softened his heart to be sensitive to those callings.

Jim's story is truly testimony that God's purposes are fulfilled in ordinary lives, ordinary settings, with ordinary people. God does not call the equipped to serve, but equips the called. I'm thankful that Jim answered those frequent calls, and that now his story can be read by many who may be questioning their purpose in life.

It's been said that we "find what we're looking for". I believe when we take the focus off of ourselves, and look to God, we will find Him. Jim looked. And, he found God's presence in even the smallest and mundane details of life in a small rural Illinois village. And now, God rewards us all in the form of Jim's reflections upon 82 years of life.

FOREWORD

Those reflections assure us that God cares about the details of each life – of each personal sojourn under the sun – and also that yes, God was indeed there during each phase of his life. Jim's story provides hope and promise to each of us. While his sojourn is not over, his story is worth telling now. And worth reading. I trust you'll find it as encouraging as I have. And I'm confident you'll also take heart in recognizing, that yes indeed, God is present! Just as He is with each of us.

Happy travels as you sojourn with Him.
william d mayo

ACKNOWLEDGEMENTS

As God has authored my life story, in a very real sense He has authored this book, as well. I am eternally grateful for the experiences, people, circumstances, and opportunities he has woven into the fabric of my life. Dark days and days of joy are a part of every human pathway, and mine is no different. But I can attest with full assurance that God "meant it all for good". His sovereign design for my life dictates that first and foremost, I must acknowledge Him with thanks for the gift of life, the blessings to serve, and the privilege to recount my journey.

I must likewise thank my dear wife Carolyn. Not only has she stood alongside with unwavering support during this project, but also through sixty years of marriage. She has provided the solid footing I needed to navigate life's path and respond to God's calling. She has been my most trusted advisor and partner, and I am immensely grateful she traveled this journey with me.

My five wonderful children – Becky, Joan, Andy, Jackie and Sara – have brought immeasurable blessings throughout my lifetime, and their steadfast support and encouragement in this endeavor have inspired me.

I want to similarly express my deep thanks to William D. Mayo, a friend and fellow believer who helped me in refining and editing my story. His help was both vital and generously provided.

Finally, I want to thank my readers. My hope is that the story of my sojourn offers hope and promise to each of you. I have no doubt that wherever you are in life, God has a purpose and calling uniquely designed for you. I hope you find inspiration to step out in faith to respond to His call.

ACKNOWLEDGEMENTS

As God has authored my life story, in a very real sense He has authored this book, as well. I am eternally grateful for the experiences, people, circumstances, and opportunities he has woven into the fabric of my life. Dark days and days of joy are a part of every human pathway, and mine is no different. But I can attest with full assurance that God "meant it all for good". His sovereign design for my life dictates that first and foremost, I must acknowledge Him with thanks for the gift of life, the blessings to serve, and the privilege to recount my journey.

I must likewise thank my dear wife Carolyn. Not only has she stood alongside with unwavering support during this project, but also through sixty years of marriage. She has provided the solid footing I needed to navigate life's path and respond to God's calling. She has been my most trusted advisor and partner, and I am immensely grateful she traveled this journey with me.

My five wonderful children – Becky, Joan, Andy, Jackie and Sara – have brought immeasurable blessings throughout my lifetime, and their steadfast support and encouragement in this endeavor have inspired me.

I want to similarly express my deep thanks to William D. Mayo, a friend and fellow believer who helped me in refining and editing my story. His help was both vital and generously provided.

Finally, I want to thank my readers. My hope is that the story of my sojourn offers hope and promise to each of you. I have no doubt that wherever you are in life, God has a purpose and calling uniquely designed for you. I hope you find inspiration to step out in faith to respond to His call.

INDEX

INTRODUCTION xv
MY ARRIVAL 1
HANNA CITY 3
SIBLINGS 7
HOMESTEAD 15
SCHOOL DAYS 19
    Elementary Years 19
    High School Years 23
POST HIGH SCHOOL 31
UNITED SATATES NAVY 35
THE ONE 41
CAREER 45
GOD – EARLY ENCOUNTERS 49
IT'S TIME 55
CALLED TO SERVE 59
PRISON MINISTRY 67
YOUTH FARM 71

PULPIT SUPPLY PREACHERS 75

HOSPITAL MINISTRY 79

PEORIA RESCUE MISSION 85

PERHAPS, ONE FINAL MINISTRY 95

FINAL REFLECTIONS 99

APPENDIX 103

INTRODUCTION

Recently, on a bright Fall day, I was visiting a friend, just swapping stories on his front porch as we typically do. When out of the blue, he said quite seriously, "Jim, you should write a book!" It set me back a little, because honestly, I had secretly often thought that I'd like to do just that.

After a long pause I admitted, "Well, yes, I'd like to tackle that, but I have no idea where or how to begin."

He smiled and simply said, "The best way to write is just to begin writing."

Now, several months later, I've managed to put a life time of memories on paper. There is nothing particularly remarkable about my story. But as I've gotten older, I've become more reflective. And more importantly, those reflections have included the realization of how God has worked throughout the entire arc of my life's journey. Sometimes without me; often times with me. And sometimes, in spite of me.

By the Grace of God, I *have* lived a long life – I'm currently 82 years old. As hard as it is for me to fathom, I've been on God's journey for over eight decades! You might question why I'd want to tell the story of my life – or even more relevant (as I have questioned) "Why would anyone want to read the story of my life?"

Very simply, while we like to think "we're in charge" in this earthly life, we are not. I see so many proofs of God's providence in the trajectory of my sojourn. And, I want to share it.

Scripture tells us in Ephesians 2:10:

> "For we are his workmanship, created in Christ Jesus for good works, which God prepared beforehand, that we should walk in them." (ESV)

I'm not claiming to be fully aligned with God's purposes throughout my lifetime. Sometimes, my journey often strayed into the wilderness of self. But I have seen how God can *and does* use anyone. *IF* we submit to His leading, even a car salesman like myself can be used to fulfill His purposes.

❦ MY ARRIVAL ❦

Mom and Dad Isbell lived in an old two story house on Third street in Hanna City, IL. Hanna City was (and still is) a small village ten miles west of Peoria, Illinois on State Route 116. Although its population was a mere six hundred residents at the time, the town still had its predictable economic strata. Some people "Had", some "Had a Little", and of course there were the "Have Nots". My family belonged in the latter mix.

I was born in our house in 1941. I was welcomed into an already large and blended family. My mom had been married before and had two daughters (Lavonne and Rose). She also had a son from her first marriage (Danny) that died at birth My dad had also been married before and had a daughter (Geri) and a son (Dick). Another brother, Wayman Thomas Isbell, was born two years prior to my arrival, however he died of complications.

With the sadness of two prior children passing, naturally, my mom was very protective of me. My half-sister Lavonne (nicknamed Vonnie) also cared for me like I was her own. Since Mom was 41 when I showed up, Vonnie's help was a huge blessing to Mom. Vonnie said that she and brother Dick were "kicked out of the house" when I was about to be born. They were sent next door to Mom's sister's house – Aunt Lorena. They watched out the window for any sign of birth. The midwife could not come for some reason, so Grandma Holt (Lillian) came over and served as midwife. After I was born, Vonnie and Dick could come back to our house and see me.

Reflections...

The Bible says, "We are fearfully and wonderfully made"… Psalm 139:14 (ESV). The question we all wrestle with is "why"? Why am I here? What is my purpose? "? How is God revealed in His creation of new life on this earth? I hope to illustrate the answers to these questions as my life's sojourn unfolds across these pages. Upon my arrival, all I can say is He created me for His purposes – unknown as they were at the time.

Such was my entry into the world. Not born into status or wealth. No modern hospital. Modest, small town environment. But with much anticipation and willing hearts to care for me. God had provided a loving family, and my journey began.

❦ *HANNA CITY* ❦

As I said, despite its size, there were still three distinct groups in our tiny village – the "haves", the "have a littles", and the "have nots". The circumstances and trappings of those three groups become apparent in the eyes of a boy. Even when we don't know what we're looking for, we are still comparing to see where we fit in. It's funny what children see and how they interpret things. The opinions we form in our early years can stick around for a lifetime. Even if not true – perception becomes reality – my reality, right or wrong.

We lived next door to mom's sister Lorena and her husband Jimmy Bradshaw. Mom's bachelor brother Walter Holt lived with the Bradshaw's. Grandma Lillian Holt also lived there – I think the house was actually hers. She died when I was five. I only remember an old white-haired lady sitting in a big oversized white wooden lawn chair in the backyard—the chair was oversized, not Grandma.

Our home didn't have a basement, indoor plumbing, a telephone, and needless to say, our toilet consisted of an outhouse about forty feet away from the backdoor just past the two cherry trees and the large garden. Dad planted tomatoes, potatoes, lettuce, corn, carrots, and green beans. And importantly, he fixed our outhouse so it could not be tipped over! He had two 2' x 8' boards bolted on opposite sides and set deep into holes so that it was solidly planted.

We got our water from a well with a hand pump that was only seven feet from the backdoor. There was a cup by the pump because sometimes you needed to prime the pump by pouring a cup of water down the top. Weekly baths came from a large wash tub filled with the well water carried into the house. Of course, it was not heated. As I said, it was modest environment!

As was Hannah City. Our village had two churches, two taverns, two grocery stores, and four gas stations. We had a Skelly gas station, a Standard gas station, a Texaco gas station that also sold radios and televisions, and a Phillips 66 station. The Phillips 66 gas was advertised to contain Diisopropyl (how can I still remember that name?) They advertised you could put "a Tiger in your tank". That very catchy phrase accompanied by a cartoon tiger stuck with me. As did the fact that there was no swing in front of the gas station.

Our little town also had other interesting spots. Rice's grocery store – where I could buy penny candy. My usuals were Halloway all-day caramel suckers and gum with baseball cards. Later when I went to High school in Farmington, ten miles west, we caught the school bus in front of Rice's store.

Kepler's tavern was another prominent landmark. There was a large back room where they showed movies, usually western's on Thursday nights. There was also a continuing series, I remember Lash Larue and Zorro, from week to week. The Bitner's – a family from Glasford, (another small town just a few miles away) – came and showed the movies. They also sold popcorn and soda. Advertising from local merchants helped defray the overhead costs. The filmed ads featuring local merchants were hilarious, much like many locally produced commercials of today The people were moving and waving very fast—so comical and unnatural. Yet, everyone knew the characters and enjoyed watching their fifteen minutes of fame flash across the screen.

Vogelsang's Standard Station was another favorite spot. It was just down the street from our home, on the corner of 3rd Street and Route 116. It was the only station with a bench swing in front. The bathroom, of course, was an outhouse in the back of the station. We'd buy sodas for a dime and bags of peanuts for five cents each. We'd sit out front on the bench, pour the peanuts into the RC, and would shake it up, drinking the cola and peanuts together. Then, we'd stare out at the road trying to guess the brand of the next car coming into town. Exciting stuff for small town boys – which usually included my friends Jimmy Rudledge, Bill Rafferty, and Elmer Vogelsang. Elmer's dad owned the station.

I can still see the gas-war signs by the road: fifteen cents a gallon. In those days, a station attendant would pump your gas, check the oil, and check the fan belt. "Connie", (Conrad), who worked there told us kids that the Gates Fan Belt Company would send a mystery shopper once in a while to see if attendants were checking the fan belts. If he did, the Gates rep would shell out five dollars.

One more off-color memory of Voglesang's… a few years later we would see a blonde girl driving a pink Ford convertible, and she would often stop by the station. Connie would eagerly rush out to wash the windshield for her. Later, we understood why as Connie told us she would spread her legs apart while he looked in the windshield! Cheap thrills!

Reflections…

When I was younger, I always lamented my poor background. It's difficult to compare one's self to others and find yourself lacking. Material possessions, status, even clothes tended to distinguish between kids. As I've grown older, I am very thankful for my humble roots. Privilege makes it more tempting to rely upon self. And I've learned that self is the enemy of God. I'm grateful none of that was in my way. I'm reminded of the Biblical passage that notes "it is easier for a camel to go through the eye of a needle than for a rich man to enter the Kingdom of Heaven."

⚜ SIBLINGS ⚜

Brother Dick

My brother Dick was the oldest of my siblings and 13 years my senior when I was born. He joined the Navy at age eighteen, when I was just five years old. He did Basic Training on the West Coast and was assigned to Hawaii after that. After he came home from the Navy, he got married. He became my Boy Scout troop leader, my fishing instructor, and later still, he even became my Sunday school teacher, Despite our age difference, though you might expect he'd want nothing to do with a runt little brother, Dick was very generous with his time.

He would, many times, pick me up on Fridays and we would go to a farm pond and seine for minnows and crawfish. These were our bait to fish for catfish. Dick would take me to Spoon River, and we would fish all night. We always took a big bag of Mom's oatmeal cookies and a couple bottles of soda. We'd pack up our sleeping bags, and scout the shore line for some strong branches to serve as our bank poles.

Dick had made a small plywood boat and we'd move up and down the river setting bank poles with strong string and hooks attached. After baiting all the lines, we would head back to a sandbar where we had set up camp and feast on cookies while slugging down sodas. We would check our lines every hour or so, and with good luck, we'd return home the next morning with a big batch of catfish.

During one such adventure, as we crawled in our sleeping bags for the night, Dick bolted from his bag hollering "Snake! Snake!". A snake had crawled into his bag while we were running our lines. Just one of the hazards of fishing all night on the river. I will never forget the fun we had and my brother's laugh as we went down the river with him wearing his old Navy hat and smoking his cigarette. Because of him, there was never any doubt that I would one day join the Navy, too.

Dick also took me squirrel hunting. He handed me a twelve gauge shotgun, stationed me on a strategic hillside, and told me to quietly watch for squirrels . He took up another position further ahead to my right. After a brief period, I did see an animal come out from under a tree – much too big for a squirrel, and I was sure it was not a dog. I took aim and fired.

It was a fox ,and it screamed like a girl when hit. Honestly, it made my hair stand up in shock and sadness. That was my first and last animal shoot. Never again. The county had a five dollar cash award for fox ears, so brother Dick made me carry that poor dead fox all the way back to the car. We turned in the fox, and I did receive my five dollars. Although I'm not sure what Dick got for the fur. Still, no amount of cash would erase the sadness of killing that wild animal, and I never hunted again.

Dick continued to trap and hunt all winter with my dad. They'd hunt mink, racoons, and muskrats. These furs were readily purchased by the local fur dealer in Farmington, Illinois. The racoon meat was sold to taverns along Lincoln Avenue in Peoria. Mom didn't drive so the two of us would wait in the car for dad to come out—sometimes it was a long wait for his "sales call". I tried to remember how to shift gears just in case he had too much to drink and I might have to drive home. I was about ten years old at the time.

Dad, my brother Dick, and Dick's two oldest son's, Gary and Randy loved to go trapping. Dad tried to get me interested but when he went to check to see if he caught anything that day, it was nighttime and very dark in the woods. He carried a .22 revolver and a flashlight, but I only had a flashlight. I was young and scared in the woods at night. I kept hearing animal sounds and felt like eyes were looking at me from the bushes and trees. He tried to assure me that we were the most freighting animal in the woods. Maybe for him that was true, but not for me. I think that was my first trip and my last checking traps. I enjoyed fishing, but not hunting or trapping.

My brother and his sons had a better relationship with Dad than I did because they liked hunting and trapping. Baseball and basketball were my sports. Dad came to watch me play basketball in grade school, but he didn't come to any baseball or basketball games during my high school years. Looking back, I realize that I should have taken more of an interest in what Dad liked to do. That is one of the things I wish I could do over.

Reflections

Brother Dick was a true friend, and given our age difference, I still marvel at the time and attention he gave to me. His camaraderie was important in those early years of my life. And while I inferred that my father liked to down a few beers as he dropped off our furs to sell, I want to make it clear he was still a good example. It was only much later in life that I came to understand him.

My dad's father left his wife and children (four boys and two daughters) and pursued a sinful life of infidelity and self. My dad had to quit school in the 5th grade to look for a job to support his family. Still, while the example of a good father was almost totally lacking in his childhood, my Dad did a very good job instilling honesty in his children. He was also a good provider. He would grow or hunt for most of our food. There were food stamps to allow for sugar and a few other things, but no government handouts—Dad would not have accepted them anyway. We usually had chuck roast or fried chicken for Sunday dinner and something from the wild during the week, such as squirrels, rabbits, fish, turtles, or frog legs. I remember squirrel legs were like trying to eat beef jerky, very tough.

Being raised the way I was taught me valuable lessons – to not rely on others for what you need, but to work hard to provide for yourself and others. That has served me well throughout my lifetime. Both dominant male figures, Brother Dick and my father, were examples that shaped my values of hard work, honesty, friendship, and masculine love. Reflecting upon their roles in my life, I have a tremendous appreciation for both, and thank God that He blessed me with these men as key influencers in my growing up years.

Sister Geri:

Geri (Geraldine) was Dick's biological sister and she lived with us only on weekends. Throughout the week, she lived with her mother in the area of Hanna City called the patch. The patch was the poorest side of town. Her Mother made Geri come stay at our home on the weekends; freeing herself to date other men. I didn't get to spend much time with Geri, but I've seen several pictures of her holding me when I was a baby. She was 10 years older than me. Her mother eventually remarried and Geri spent most time with her and her new husband, Harry. I remember when Geri got married. She had Harry give her away instead of my Dad. He was deeply hurt. I know it was her mom's doing. I also know that when my Dad died—Geri didn't attend his funeral. She admitted to me later that her mom didn't tell her that Dad had died. How sad! Bitterness proves to be a very difficult pill to swallow and even harder to digest. Sometimes, very sadly, it simply lingers in the system, and never fully goes away.

Geri was married to Dale Jones, a school teacher and coach. Dale was good to me and came by a few Saturdays to take me to the Peoria YMCA to play basketball. Dale was a good looking guy and a sharp dresser. His personality was totally unlike anyone else in our family. I guess that I wasn't terribly surprised when Dale and Geri got divorced. Geri found out that Dale was having an affair with her best friend from work.

I did get to spend time with Geri much later in California, where she worked for one of the big airplane companies on the Saturn Space program. And much later, Geri and her new husband Marvin took my wife and I to Palm Springs, California for a few days.

Reflections

While my memories of Geri have grown dim over the years, I still believe God provided important life lessons for me from our relationship. I learned of the destructive force of bitterness; the challenge of avoiding temptation that can destroy relationships, and also that time (and a willing heart) can salve old hurts. God is not beyond any one's reach – try as we might to distance ourselves from Him. Nothing can separate us from His love.

Sister Rose:

Roselle was Lavonne's biological sister and my half-sister. I didn't get to know Rose very much at all. Rose was seven years older than Lavonne and was living on her own when I was born. She worked at Caterpillar. When my Mom got divorced, Rose went to live with her dad while Lavonne stayed to live my mom. Rose was in my eyes mature and sophisticated, but I truly did not know her.

Reflections

It saddens me to realize I didn't have a well-developed relationship with Rose. But God still taught me the challenges that broken homes can wreak on a small child. I'm convinced this was a lesson that served me well in my own family as I grew into the man God had designed me to be.

Sister Lavonne:

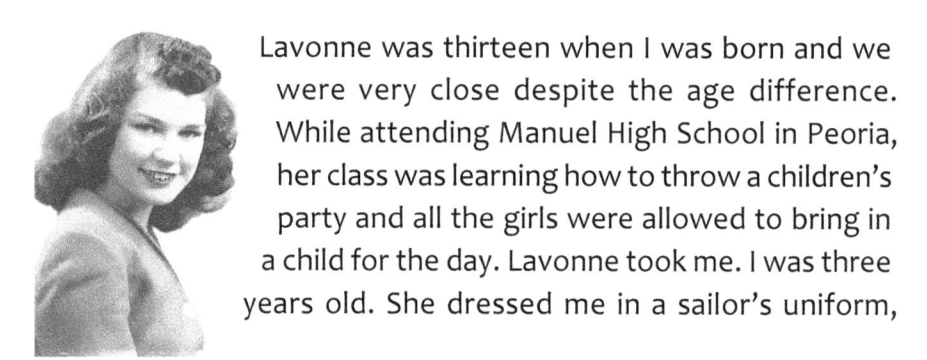

Lavonne was thirteen when I was born and we were very close despite the age difference. While attending Manuel High School in Peoria, her class was learning how to throw a children's party and all the girls were allowed to bring in a child for the day. Lavonne took me. I was three years old. She dressed me in a sailor's uniform, which she probably made. Vonnie said I was the only boy brought to school that day, so I was a big hit.

I was five when Vonnie graduated and she had several girlfriends show up at our house many times over the years – so they all knew me. After High School, Lavonne worked at Crawford's Shoe Store across the street from the courthouse in Peoria. When Mom and I would ride the bus to Peoria, we would almost always visit Crawford's to see Lavonne. I remember the machine they had where you could put your feet in and look down to see your correct size. I believe it was some kind of x-ray machine. There was a boy that worked there also, and he bought me a cap gun. I suspect he was trying to impress my sister. Vonnie once took me down the street to the Downy Flake restaurant and bought me a hot chocolate and a donut. Funny how that stands out in my memory. It was a cold day and also the day that Santa Claus came to town in Peoria for the big parade.

Lavonne was a great story teller. She told me about my first dog—a dog named Scotty. I was only three and couldn't get the "S" out—so I called him Cotty. Vonnie said that Mom didn't worry about me when I was outside because I had my hand on Scotty's back and he would not leave my side.

One sad day, Vonnie took me and Scotty with her to the grocery store in Hanna City which was about three blocks east of home, but across Route 116. As we were coming home, Scotty ran ahead for some reason. He was hit by a car and killed. Vonnie said I kept calling Cotty, Cotty, Cotty all the way home.

Lavonne could roller skate quite well, and sometimes took me along to the Fernwood Roller Rink just outside of Peoria. That's where I learned to roller skate.

Reflections...

Vonnie was no doubt a positive influence on my young life. I have many sweet memories of her – some first hand, and some I learned from her. She definitely had a big interest in me and in my life. Still today, despite her advanced age, she continues to teach me and share memories of my childhood. What stands out about this remarkable sister is her unconditional love, her kindness, and her continual attentiveness to me. It could probably go without saying, but she is a believer, and the love of Christ was on full display in her life. I'm so thankful for God's provision of Vonnie throughout my sojourn on this earth. What a gift! She is now 95, lives by herself, has a heart pacemaker, and just survived colon cancer with chemo treatments. A real trouper with a great memory.

❧ *HOMESTEAD* ❧

I was five years old when my Dad had a local Farmington company raise our house and dig a basement underneath. With this upgrade, we finally graduated to an indoor bathroom, and all the other indoor plumbing benefits. Wow, what a difference that made! We could take a bath or shower with warm water. If there was a drawback, it was that we now had to buy toilet paper — the old Sears catalog pages just wouldn't work anymore.

The other big upgrade at this time was that we installed a coal furnace with an auger to feed the coal into it. We got rid of the pot belly stove that stood in the dining room. My arm was burnt badly once when I was pushed up against it during a Cub Scout meeting, so I definitely did not miss that thing!

The only bad part about the new furnace was that there was only one heat register for the entire house. Any heat for the three upstairs bedrooms was the heat that percolated up the stairs from that single register. Winters were very cold. The windows were single pane glass, paper thin, and when the wind blew and it snowed; snow would make a small pile inside my room. I remember having at least seven blankets on my bed. In the summer, Dad bought two window fans, one for upstairs and one for downstairs. They helped, but it was still hot.

During winter time, my job was to shovel coal from the coal room, which was right next to the furnace, into the hopper so the auger could feed the coal into the furnace. Dad had a long tool to reach into the furnace for removing the clinkers. Coal contains moisture along with other mineral impurities that break down inside the furnace, mixing together. This created debris resembled lava rocks. Clinkers made the furnace less efficient, and they needed to be busted up into small cinders. My job was to break them up and carry them out to the driveway. Our driveway was dirt and mud most of the time, so it was to my advantage to bust up the clinkers finely as they became my basketball court.

Before we had that basement, we had a fruit cellar. It was a small, dug out room under the house with a dirt floor. This was where mom kept mason jars of tomatoes and other fruit that she canned. An outside wooden door that folded over the opening and a few stairs was the only entryway. I can still recall that very musty smelling place; it was spooky, smelly, and I didn't like it one bit!

The garage in the back of the house was big enough to hold our car, a 1938 Plymouth, and a large metal box (part of an old refrigerator) that held my dad's hunting traps. Once, while Dad was getting some traps out of that metal box, a rat jumped out, ran up Dad's leg and out the side of his bib overalls! That frightening episode made that room even more of a fearsome place!

Reflections

Dad also had a workbench and shelves to hold things in that garage. I remember seeing his helmet and a carbide light that was attached to his helmet from his coal mining days. His lunch bucket was there also—it was tall and round and all the miners had the same kind. It was his "uniform". I learned that to do a job well, one had to be prepared with the proper "armor". Little did I realize however, that God was also preparing me for the day I would don my life's armor – the "helmet" of Salvation and the Light of God's Word. While that day was coming, I wasn't able to fully perceive it then. But still, I did sense God's hand upon me.

✧ SCHOOL DAYS ✧

Elementary Years

Starting grade school was a learning experience in more than the expected ways. I was newly exposed to things I really had not experienced before. We started each day by standing outside facing the American flag, placing our hand over our heart and saying the pledge of allegiance. Our country was united having just come through the bombing of Pearl Harbor by the Japanese. Being united was a good feeling. I remember a sense of standing up for the good of all people, and feeling that God was on our side.

I remember my first day of school. We went outside for recess and I loved the sliding board and swings. I had a new ball cap on, and a girl named Judy said she liked it. Then, a boy named Dave Rowden, who lived by the school, knocked my hat off. I punched him on the nose. He started bleeding and crying, and I took off for home. Nothing came from that in terms of discipline or punishment, but he stayed away from me from that day forward. Actually, I learned something else. I felt bad for hitting him.

Our first and second grade teacher was an older lady named Ethel Cook. She was very strict. Chewing gum seemed to really set her off. (I wondered… Didn't she ever chew gum?) If we needed to use the bathroom we had to raise our hand and she would ask if we needed number one or number two. I guess she wanted to know how long we would be gone, as if she could put a time limit on such things.

I missed some time from school because of various bouts with childhood illnesses. I had the measles, chicken pox, and mumps, and as a result, I missed the lesson on telling time. I had to teach myself how to tell time. I did this without telling anyone, because I was too embarrassed at not knowing how.

Some kids were cruel and made fun of others. We had a mildly retarded girl in our class named Patsy. She talked funny and slobbered some and became the object of cruel remarks. While I felt sorry for her, I didn't stand up for her – and I still feel badly about that. I also remember wondering what had happened to her to cause her issues. I didn't understand that she, too, was made for a purpose in bringing glory to God.

The grade school had four rooms with two grades in each room. It was always nice to move up to a new room. That meant a new teacher and the feeling of growing up. My third and fourth grade teacher, Mrs. Collins, would read a chapter out of the Hardy Boys Mystery books after lunch each day, and I became hooked. I also loved books on horses and dogs, such as *Black Beauty* and *Call of the Wild*.

In the seventh and eighth grades, we got our first male teacher, Mr. Gibbs. He also became our school principal. He started a softball team and a basketball team. We didn't have a gym, just a blacktop open-air court in back of the school, so we played our basketball games in the neighboring town of Farmington at its Junior High School gym.

Mr. Gibbs successfully lobbied to get a new gym and two classrooms added to the back of the school. It did not have a wooden floor court, just vinyl tile, but it was an indoor gym just the same. The gym was opened when I was in eighth grade. We even had cheerleaders. I don't know who selected them, but in our boyhood eyes, they were the prettiest girls in the school. All except one – but we boys thought that was fine as she had big boobs that made up for looks. They bounced up and down when she cheered. It seemed to fascinate all of us.

Mr. Gibbs took five of us boys with him to his hometown of Biggsville, for a week-end during his town's Centennial Celebration. That was a big deal to be asked to go along. I was excited to attend.

Baseball was also a big focus of mine. Our ball diamond was on the west side of the school and the swings were on the east side along with a sliding board. The ball field always looked so big —but later I realized just how small it was. I thought I was hitting the ball a long way. A teammate named Jack Scheckler, who batted left-handed, could hit it out of the park. It wasn't as far as I thought but at the time, I thought that was Major League!

Dad had bought me a first baseman's ball glove at Sears when I was in the 4th grade, so I became the first baseman. Jim Monroe was the catcher, Jack Schekler was on third, Jerry Lonsberry was the shortstop, and my friend, Steve Turbett was the second baseman. They were popular guys and now I was one of them. They were counting on me at first base (or at least I thought so).

I remember being at the baseball field in Hanna City over by the sportsman club where the Sunday morning men's league played. They had finished a practice session and I was on hand, having ridden there on my bike with my ever present ball glove slung over the handlebars.

Dutch Schultz, who lived down our street, saw me standing there with my glove on. The men's team was done with practice, so he directed me to third base and began to hit me some grounders. I noticed my Uncle Stobert by the fence. He was watching. I got excited that someone was watching me play, and while I was never around Uncle Stobert much at all, it was still thrilling to have an audience. It must have inspired me, because no matter how hard Dutch hit those balls, I fielded them all. I saw Uncle Stobert smile. And that is a moment of joy that I still remember.

Reflections

I suppose we all want an audience and the approval of others. Funny how Uncle Stobert provided that for me at that time, and how I relished his approval. I'm reminded of Scripture's admonition in 2 Timothy 2:15: "Do your best to present yourself to God as one approved, a worker who has no need to be ashamed, rightly handling the word of truth." I certainly didn't realize it at the time, but God would be tossing me some hot grounders one day, and I pray that He has approved of my fielding.

❦ SCHOOL DAYS ❦

High School Years

I attended High School in Farmington, Illinois, another small town which was about ten miles west of Hanna City. Coal mining and farming were the main industries of the day in the Farmington area. I was entering a new school with new teachers and many new students. My world was getting considerably bigger, and It was both exciting and a bit intimidating. Many Farmington residents were of Italian descent, and most were from coal mining families. I won't say this was a rough crowd, but it was quite different and new to me. It felt as if I were entering a radically new environment.

The first day of school started with Home Room, which was also a new concept to us. I don't remember much teaching going on there, but I do recall one episode when Mrs. Lawner – the home room teacher – left the room for a few minutes. A Farmington boy named Dave got up, went over to the second story window, opened the window and threw out all the books from her desk. We small town farm kids who were bussed in from tiny Hanna City or other small towns and rural areas collectively shuddered. This was certainly my first exposure to open rebellion against authority, and I was shell-shocked. When she came back and saw what had happened, no one said a word. Without intending to, we had just joined the rebellion.

The thought comes to me now, "If you don't stand for something, you'll fall for anything!'

Classes were in different rooms which was also unique from grade school. When the bell rang it was time to go to the next room for the next class. My expectations and anxiety created a bit of instability. My emotions were all over the place, especially after that home room class.

I was looking forward to trying out for the basketball team because I was very good in grade school, and I had played and worked on shots at home for years and especially over the summer before high school. But, it seemed that the Farmington coach, Mr. Stinson had his mind made up before the tryouts even started. I didn't make the team.

I had to satisfy myself by playing basketball over the lunch hour with some of the other guys. When the football coach, Walt Grebe, saw Gary McDonald and me playing – he approached us and asked why we were both not on the team. When we told him we had been cut—he said, "I will have a talk with Stinson about that."

The next year Gary and I were on the team. We didn't get to play a whole lot, maybe it was because Coach Stinson was forced to put us on the team. I got a taste of politics, injustice, favoritism, and revenge all at once. It stands out in my memory – not in a good way.

Baseball in the spring was a different matter. Walt Grebe, the football coach was also the baseball coach, and I didn't have any problem making the team. Coach Grebe was a great coach, but some of the others should have stayed teaching driver training or science class. Some people, I learned, just cannot lead or coach others.

Girls were an entirely different matter. It seemed that the girls were most interested in locking in a guy to "go steady" with them. They did not want the guys to be "playing the field." The first girl that locked me in was named Sharon. We didn't talk much and never went on a date. How could I? I lived twelve miles away and had no car or driver's license. "Going steady" simply meant that I was not to be seen with any other girl. Upon reflection, while harmless I suppose, this silly ritual was fueled by a naiveite, complete lack of knowledge, and no advice from home.

I was a kid that didn't ask a lot of questions. I just assumed that if I needed to know something my parents would tell me. That was a big mistake and that didn't always work out well. I didn't know what I didn't know. My niece, Lavonne's oldest daughter Cathy, told me later that Aunt Lorena told her lots of stuff. My Mom was more the quiet type so I didn't learn much about family matters or social conventions. In a way, I was navigating life without a good compass.

The reality is that the only goals I had in high school were to play sports and graduate. Sports were my life. But, I knew that college would be out of the question because we didn't have money for that. I didn't even consider asking my parents. It would just make them feel badly about their limited means. It was hard enough to ask for a suit so I could go to one of the dances. They never came to any games, and I can't remember if they even came to my graduation. What a far cry difference from the hovering parents of today. Good or bad? I'm not sure a blanket statement can be made. Simply put, it was just a different time.

I never smoked in school—but I did drink with the guys. And, to my shame, I also tried to get in girls' pants like most boys in high school. I was not perfect. And I am not very proud of that. Some might call this a normal "rite of passage" or typical hijinks and hormones of a teenage boy. But what it really reveals is the self-absorption of my own sinful nature. Innocence lost. The battle of self-will was raging inside and I was either oblivious to it or a willing conspirator.

I certainly had many good friends in high school, but must admit that several of the guys from Farmington were rough and mean. I recall one incident when following post-game showers , a boy next to me was drying off when one of the rough guys took a brush out of the "tuf-skin" bowl and swiped it in that boy's butt crack. Tuf-Skin is a common product for athletes. It reduces friction and blisters. However, it is made from isopropyl alcohol; rosin; butane; and propane! it stings like the dickens when applied. Burns might be a better word! And it is definitely not intended for use between the butt cheeks! It could take days to wear off when used normally. That boy no doubt would never forget that episode!

Another time a boy came out of the shower and was immediately shoved out the door to the playing field completely naked! Of course, the girls were coming toward their locker room door after their practice! No mercy! Sad how people always take advantage of the most vulnerable among us. Sadly, this continues long into adulthood – it just takes different forms!

Social life in high school often centered on homecoming games and regular dances. These were always a big deal. For one particular dance, I had a date with a girl named Sandy . I had no idea what was expected of me. I did not get her a flower or pick her up at her home. Again, my parents didn't attempt to advise on such trivial issues. Mrs. Turbett, a neighbor lady, kindly drove us to Farmington and dropped us off at the dance. As I went inside, someone asked me where Sandy was. I dashed outside and stopped Mrs. Turbett before she drove away. Luckily, I did know where Sandy lived. Mrs. Turbett drove me to her home to pick her up. I didn't have a flower for her to wear. I was definitely not a sophisticated date! Ignorance was no defense. Yes, I could have and should have thought to ask someone. But, to my great shame and embarrassment, I didn't even think about that. I was just naïve, and learned a tough and embarrassing lesson. Oh, by the way… that was also my first and last date with Sandy!

Even though Farmington was a good sized town compared with Hanna City, not much exciting ever happened. Its Main street boasted a local soda fountain and drug store that also had a few pinball machines. I cannot remember the name of the store. I liked the lime drinks, but had no money to play the pinball machines, so I was a mere spectator. The guys that smoked would lay their cigarettes down on the marble countertop while they played. I watched their cigarettes burn down to the nub, and a small pool of tar would form. I decided right then and there that I wanted no part of smoking or deposits of tar inside of my lungs!

There was also a movie theater in Farmington and a bowling alley. We had neither in Hanna City, so those establishments became the places to go – both with the guys and later, when I had a car, on dates.

One enduring mystery, which might be called exciting, occurred during my High School years. A local wealthy man named Faye Rawley, disappeared under questionable circumstances in 1953. There was a great deal of coal "strip-mining" in our area in those years and a local sheriff named Virgil Ball was convinced that he knew whomever killed the millionaire buried him inside his 1953 Cadillac in one of those strip-mine pits. The search dragged on for years, but every time they dug a new hole looking for that Cadillac, no car or body was ever found. The mystery was never solved. Ironically, when school administration wanted to know which students drove to school and what kind of car they had, sign-up sheets were passed around for each of us to register. Boys being boys, the most listed name and car was (you guessed it) - Faye Rawley and his 1953 Cadillac!

Actually, I rode the bus to school almost all the time. First, I had no car, but later, when I did have a car—there was no money for gas. The only jobs for kids in Hanna City was farm work during the summers. I helped bale hay and straw for a dollar an hour. I enjoyed working on the wagon behind the tractor and baler, but not working in the loft of the barn. It was hot and lots of dust as the bales were hoisted into that space.

Football games drew crowds and sometimes ended in a fight with the other team's crowd. Especially when we played Canton and Pekin. I stayed out of those conflicts. I wanted friends, not fights. I didn't then and I still don't see how violence resolves anything.

My cousin Roger, uncle Earl's boy, had polio when he was in grade school and they did not give him a very good chance of walking again, but by the time he got to high school, he was the full back on the football team. He had no fear of getting hurt. He was two years older than me, and with every injury he suffered, my chances of playing football increased. But it didn't happen as my mom simply wouldn't give her permission.

One friend, Bob Fontana, started dating a girl named Judy Vernon, who was in my grade school class. Bob worked at the local grocery store in Farmington and always had a smile on his face. We became good friends. After we graduated from High school, Bob and Judy got married. Very good people. I wish we would have kept in close contact for they were my kind of people.

The guys who lived on farms could afford nice cars while the rest of us did without or drove old clunkers. Clothes in high school were not a problem—boys all wore jeans and a white t-shirt. My jeans always came from Penney's, the "Foremost" brand. Levi's were the status brand. I never owned a pair.

I don't remember anyone giving us advice on what classes to sign up for, but I am glad that I did take a typing class—I had no idea how important that would become. There was a girl named Wanda Campbell, who rode the school bus with the Hanna City bunch. She lived just outside Hanna City on a farm. Wanda sat between myself and another student in typing class. When we had a timed test, one of us would reach over and spin her typewriter carriage just for mean-spirited fun. Fun for us but not for her. She was very pretty. I don't know why I never asked her for a date—I guess I thought she was out of my league. It was the same way in accounting class with another pretty girl that sat across from me. Looking back, I realize that consciously or unconsciously we classed ourselves into some conjured social strata. Our self-assessed worth and where we fell in the pecking order derived from those self-limiting assessments. "Don't reach too high–you will only be disappointed." "You are not good enough to make the team." My brother Dick must have seen that attitude in me, for he told me once, "You can be anything you want to be." I have thought of that many times in my life.

Reflections

Such self-limiting assessments often follow us for life. I believe it wasn't until I was in the Navy that I began to slowly rewrite that subconscious script. While still in High School, a friend named Leonard Williams and I joined the Naval Reserve and went to meetings in East Peoria. We were never together after those classes ended. We both headed off to boot camp and different paths. I went to the regular Navy, while Leonard went to the Sea Bee's – the Navy's construction battalion. Leonard chose something he could apply to real life, while I did not. In a sense, I may have been a bit envious at the practicality of his choice, versus the nebulous future that loomed before me.

But in spite of myself, for some reason I did not fully comprehend, I always had a feeling of God's presence near to me. It's as if I knew on some level that God was sovereign and my path was in His hands. I now realize that Leonard went to learn about construction, while my learning would be about life and people. In God's plan, I would become a builder, as well.... a workman building in the Kingdom of God

POST HIGH SCHOOL

Upon graduation, some of my classmates went on to college. I went to work. Geri worked in the office for Hyster in Peoria, and when I graduated, she helped me get a job there, as well. I was only seventeen when I graduated, and a person had to be at eighteen to work in a factory. Geri said to just tell them that I was eighteen! I thought perhaps the company really didn't care about my true age, because after all the information I gave them there was little doubt how old I actually was. This proved an accurate assumption, as I was hired and started working on a burr bench grinding off rough edges on machined parts. Starting pay was a whopping $2.09/hour. I was promoted later to the wash machine and soon after to driving a lift truck delivering parts to machines for the next stage in the manufacturing process.

Working the dayshift at Hyster was more to my liking. That change occurred after I was promoted to the forklift operator position. I would deliver tubs of parts for machines to the operators performing the next phase of the finished product assembly. The operators worked on production quotas, and were expected to produce the amounts required for their assigned product. Manufacturing operates like choreography, so no downstream work station wanted to be held hostage waiting on a trucker to deliver their parts. I got to meet many more people; and driving the lift truck allowed me to see the whole factory and connect faces with the different departments. I remember the day shift foreman was Jim Clayton and the supervisor was Bob Shirley. The night foreman, was Jack Short. All of them were really good men. There was another foreman or supervisor I didn't know much. His name was Pete Herron.

I'm glad I didn't interface with him very often, as he was always scowling and seemed happiest when he found someone to reprimand. No one had a good word to say about him. He was a short man. Someone said he suffered from "short man syndrome". I'm not sure what made him so gnarly, but I certainly recall his sour disposition! I think that he was so absorbed in his title, that he wanted to be the tough guy that instilled fear in everyone. Why can't people just get along and be kind to everyone? That's certainly what we are called to do in the Bible!

Hyster sponsored a bowling team and I was all over that. Anything sports-related captured my attention. I joined the fast pitch softball team, and the horseshoe pitching team, as well. I liked all of the teams and met many more employees who worked different shifts. The softball fast-pitch league was my favorite. We played games all over the Peoria area. I alternated pitching duties with a man named Harold Zanders. Most often, I played second base. I still have a picture in my mind of a game against Keystone Steel and Wire Company. It was a local company based in Bartonville.

Porky Welsh was batting. He was also from Hanna City. He batted left handed and I was playing defense on second base. He hit a hard line drive that would have cleared my head by inches, but my glove hand went up instantly, and I caught the ball barely in the webbing. Porky jumped up and down and exclaimed, "He didn't even know he caught it!" He was right! But, he was also out!

Later in life when I started reading C.S. Lewis books, I came upon a quote that is still occupies space upon my desk today. It reminds me of myself and all the people that came into my life in those years. *" Prosperity knits a man to this world. He feels that he is finding his place in it, while in reality the world is finding its place in him."*

Reflections

While driving to work one morning, I started thinking about life and wondered, "Is this all there is now… work, eat, sleep and repeat?" I was beginning to ponder some weightier questions, as well such as "Who am I?" "Where am I going? "Why am I here"? And I also remember stating out loud, "God, what do you want from me?" I guess God was nudging me a bit and He was listening to my ponderings. Soon, He began to illustrate the direction He wanted me to follow.

❦ *UNITED STATES NAVY* ❦

I eventually left my job at Hyster in order to fulfill my commitment to the US Navy that I had made during high school. Mom and Dad took me to the train station in Peoria and I traveled well north of Chicago to the Great Lakes Naval Training Center. We were issued uniforms and assigned to a unit. Our leader was a Chief Warrant Officer named Smith. He had come up through the ranks and was tough. He had us marching all the time and tried to mold us into a cohesive unit. CWO Smith had his work cut out for him.

The guy standing next to me was named Norris, and he had a big problem keeping his mouth shut. I don't mean that he talked all the time—It was simply that his mouth would hang open while he just stood there. CWO Smith came over to Norris, put his nose on Norris' nose and shouted, "What the f-xxx are you, the company Zombie? Shut your mouth." When I smiled, he asked if I had something to say? "NO, Sir!" I replied. It was quite the shock and a valuable lesson in self-control.

The men who smoked could only do so when the order, "The smoking lamp is lit" was given. I never smoked. When CWO Smith was gone for a while—he picked the biggest man in the company to be in charge. A guy from New York wanted to smoke when he wasn't supposed to. He did it anyway and when challenged by the big recruit in charge told him to "go f-xxx himself."

When Smith returned and the incident was reported to him, he had an exceptionally effective solution. He ordered the New Yorker to take out his pack of smokes and, luckily for that recruit, he only had four left in the pack. Smith made him light them all and smoke them down to the butt all at the same time. Oh, I should add, CWO Smith put a bucket over his head!

In the heat of August, it was hard to stay awake in those classrooms that were boring and had no air conditioning. But everyone endured and eventually graduated. I was sent to Philadelphia awaiting assignment to a ship. While there, we were given jobs; such as being sent over to the Officer's Club to clean up after a night of partying and heavy drinking. The smell was terrible and the mess was worse. And these were men who had been appointed as "Officers and a Gentlemen" by an act of Congress! That says a lot about the officers AND about Congress, I'm afraid.

There were always seasoned sailors awaiting discharge or reassignment. They would often approach unsuspecting newbies asking to borrow a few dollars – always promising to pay them back soon. What none of us knew was the fact they were leaving the next morning. Lessons in life have to be experienced. And I learned that if you can't verify, don't trust.

Eventually, I was assigned to the U.S.S. Galveston CLG3, which was a Guided Missile Light Cruiser. The ship was 612 feet long with a company of 1200 men. I was assigned to the radar room and trained to watch screens for contact activity. It was below decks in a dark room—I hated it. I asked to be sent to the deck gang. Everyone said, "You are crazy–they really have to work up there." I didn't care about that—I just wanted to be outside and see the sunshine.

I studied hard and passed the required tests and soon became a Boatswain mate designated Seaman First Class. I now had some responsibility to direct the work of the deck hands. We went to Bayonne, New Jersey for radar repair. From there we went to Norfolk, Virginia, and then on to Mayport, Florida, followed by Jacksonville and Yorktown. While there, we on-loaded ammo and missiles. We then set sail for San Juan, Puerto Rico. After being at sea for a while, sailors were usually eager for a port visit. San Juan was just the ticket for many who went ashore to let off steam, drink voluminous quantities of booze, and for many, seek opportunities (in their words) "to get some pussy."

After that "play date" ashore, it was back to business again, and we sailed to Guantanamo, Cuba for war games. The Russians were sending missiles to communist leader Fidel Castro at that time with the implied intent to attack America. We played war games by firing the big guns and the Talos Missiles at drones positioned over one-hundred miles away. On the fantail of the ship was a huge turret that held two Talos missiles. Each one was about thirty feet long. The big guns I mentioned were in two turrets (one on each side of midships). They were 5 inch – .38 caliber guns, meaning the diameter of the projectiles fired was five inches and the barrel of the gun was nearly sixteen feet long. Forward on the ship was an even bigger turret which housed a 6 inch – .47 caliber gun. Its barrel was almost twenty-four feet long, and it fired a projectile that was six inches in diameter. Each shell and casing weighed approximately 130 pounds and these could fire that projectile a distance of over eleven miles! No doubt this likely made the Russians nervous, as indeed tensions were high. President Kennedy eventually succeeded in causing Russia to remove their missiles, and the threat of was averted.

SOJOURN

We made other ports of call on our deployment, such as Kingston, Jamaica. There was another stop we made and I can't remember its name, but the ship's Captain informed us to stay out of trouble for they would not be able to help us due to the political unrest in that region. We had to anchor off-shore and take the crew's launch to port. I was trained to run the crew's launch. As the operator, I would stand mid-point in the launch with men ahead and behind me. It was difficult to operate as the waves bounced the launch relentlessly – especially when approaching up close to the ship for boarding and off-loading sailors.

We saw firsthand what the Captain was talking about when locals would swim out to the ship wanting us to throw coins in the water for them. Some had hands missing, and we were told it was their punishment for being caught stealing. Some had both hands missing. Made us wonder what happened if they raped a woman – typical sailors, minds always in the gutter!

I mentioned that I never smoked, but cigarettes were only a dollar a carton while at sea in International Waters. Smokes were great trading bait, and when we went ashore they could be traded for just about anything. In a sense, I couldn't afford NOT to smoke!.

When my years of service were completed, I returned to Hanna City and started back to work at Hyster in Peoria. Of course, I had to buy a car. I noticed a 1958 Impala two-door hardtop on Travis Cadillac's used car lot. It was a sleek baby blue with a 348 cubic inch V-8 engine. The price was $1095.00. With 90 day interest-free terms, it was a good deal, yet that was still a lot of money for me. I bit the bullet and did buy it on terms, and I also managed to have it paid it off within 90 days. It turned out to be a good car.

The next 2 years were not my best. I always had a cooler of beer in the trunk and ran with the other young guys and veterans working at Hyster. I was pretty much still a reckless sailor during those days. I regret the way I lived – young and dumb.

At Hyster, I was eventually assigned to the assembly line building lift trucks. I worked with a Polish man who had been a prisoner of war in Russia and worked in Siberia building railroads for the Russians. He had many stories to tell. "Walt" as everyone called him for no one could pronounce his actual name, brought two thermos bottles to work every day. One was filled with coffee and the other with hot tea and vodka. The vodka, obviously, was a private matter.

Reflections…

After a year, I started to take classes at Bradley University in Peoria. I only took two at a time. Classes cost $27.00 a semester hour, and that was all I could afford while continuing to work full time. I was put on the 2nd shift driving a lift truck, so I could attend my classes in the mornings. Later, I was put in the shipping office handling all the incoming invoices. I continued shuttling back and forth to college, and as long as I kept up with my work demands at Hyster, they permitted it.

❦ THE ONE ❦

*I*t wasn't long after this, that I met a girl named Carolyn. She was in nurse's training at Methodist Hospital School of Nursing. I actually met her on a blind date with my cousin Jerry Swardenski. Jerry had just been discharged from the Army. He was in the paratroopers, but like me, returned home and began working at Hyster also. There were three of us guys and three girls on that date. It "just happened" that I walked out with Carolyn instead of one of the other girls. But I'm quite sure that "coincidence" was entirely God's doing! We got married two years later.

God was (and is) so good. All my life I had felt His presence and His hand over me—even when I was in total disobedience. The commitment I made to God at a tent meeting as a boy was still in effect – at least from God's perspective! (More about that later).

Carolyn and I lived in a small upstairs apartment next door to the Methodist Church in Morton, Illinois. Carolyn's parents were members of the Apostolic Christian Church in Morton so we attended there. We were not members so we could not get married in the church, so, to please her parents, we were married in the Elder Brother's home with only her sister Judy standing up for her and my brother Dick standing up for me. I remember the Elder, Joe A. Getz, said that we could bring two baskets of flowers. At that point, his submissive wife stuck her head around the corner and said, "Bring all the flowers you want." (The lesson I learned here was that if you watch long enough you will always find out who is in charge).

Our reception was in her parents' house on Main Street in Morton. This had been Carolyn's and her five sisters childhood home. It was a small house. People came in the front door greeted us, went through the kitchen to get a plate of food, then exited out the back door to the lawn chair reception area. It was a beautiful day.

We took our honeymoon in my 1963 Chevy Corvair, heading north toward Rockford, Illinois. We stopped in Mendota at a small motel with a restaurant next door and spent our first night there. The next day we drove on to Rockford and stayed a couple of days at the Holiday Inn. Not extravagant as we were on a self-imposed and very tight budget.

We rented a small apartment upstairs in the home of our Brother-in-law, Wayne Galbraith. Mr. Galbraith wanted to know what day I got paid, and I explained that I got paid on Friday's. He said that I should leave $15.00 a week on their kitchen table each Friday for the rent. We lived there for a year and then bought our own home a few blocks away. It cost $17,000. We had a small down payment and financed the remainder. I was feeling very grown up and with that realization came many responsibilities..

Carolyn graduated and received her RN degree. She obtained a good job in town with Dr. Eric Maran. I continued to work at Hyster and attend classes at Bradley University. When my classes were scheduled for the early afternoon, I picked up a job with a local contractor putting up drywall in the mornings. Of course, I continued working at Hyster, this time on second shift from 4:00- 11:00 PM. After a long day – each day – I would head home. The morning job only lasted a few months because it did not leave sufficient time to study. After completing thirty credit hours toward my degree from Bradley, I dropped out. I was married, with a mortgage, and only a second shift job. Life wasn't going according to MY plan. But God was at work.

About three months before I secured new employment, I received a call from my brother Dick that Dad had a heart attack and was enroute to Methodist Hospital in Peoria. Carolyn was working, and I immediately went to the hospital. When I arrived, Dad had already been assigned a hospital room, and my brother and I did get to talk with him. The last words I heard him say was, "It sure is nice to have two fine sons." Dad seemed to be doing alright and they needed someone to go down and give his information to the hospital admitting. I volunteered. By the time I got back to his room, they had asked Mom, Dick, and Lavonne to step outside the room while they worked to revive Dad. He had gone into cardiac arrest. Revival attempts were unsuccessful, and Dad passed away.

Reflections

The next few days were a blur, but after the funeral I was back at Hyster for my night job. Life and obligations go on. At supper time I took my sack lunch and went up on the roof and had a long talk with God as I stared out over the Illinois river. I felt God's peace surround me as I asked for direction and what God wanted from me.

CAREER

My focus while attending Bradley University was on earning a teaching degree. I definitely thought I was on "the right path", and I could see myself as a teacher. But it was *my* path – not necessarily God's path. Despite the issues with adequate study time, another event convinced me that path was not right after all. One of the guys working with me was also studying to become a teacher. He was scheduled to graduate with his teaching degree, and had already been hired by the local Pekin School District as teacher. He boasted that his starting salary would be $5,200 a year. Working at Hyster, I was already bringing home $6,500 a year. That was so discouraging! I thought college would pave the way to a brighter and more secure future. Instead, it felt like a step backward.

My new Mother-in-Law suggested that I find a job in sales. I'm not sure what she saw in me that prompted that suggestion, but I reflect now that it was more likely God speaking through her! I found an ad in the paper for salesmen to sell Gerber baby food . The job came with a car. That perk of a car really appealed to me – not that I wanted to sell baby food! I applied and took a test, yet the man in charge said I was overqualified for the job and projected that I would not like it.

I thought "Well, if sales is to be my path, perhaps I should sell something bigger". Bob Grimm was a local Chevrolet dealer, and not long thereafter, Carolyn ran into him at a local coffee shop. Out of the blue (yes, God must be laughing at that phrase), Bob asked her if I would like to sell cars. He wanted me to finish out the semester but I had already dropped my course of study. And, I was eager to get started. On November 1st of 1965, I began my new gig.

Car sales is a commission only salary structure, but until I got my footing, Bob Grimm generously provided $500 a month. This allowed some runway for the first few months while I learned the business. The first four months my commissions were less than the $500 dollars. But in month five, things started to come together and I made $1,300.00. I felt like I was in tall clover!

Not to focus too much on finances, but that first year I made $10,200.00 and the second year I made $12,500.00 – twice as much as I was bringing home from my Hyster job. I won't say success came easy, but I continued to work hard and God provided good results. My third year I grossed $15,000.00. I thought, "Surely I had reached the pinnacle." Then someone told me about a salesman in Peoria who made $32,000.00. So, I set my sights even higher and the next year I made $25,500.00

While at Grimm's Chevrolet, all of his sales people were required to take a test. It was called the Greenburg Aptitude Test. This assessment was developed by Herb Greenberg, PhD. Having studied under Anna Freud and Abraham Maslow, Dr. Greenberg took on the challenge to develop the Caliper Profile assessment to predict sales success of prospective sales employees. His work was published in the *Harvard Business Review*, the *New York Times*, and *Forbes*, among others. Many US businesses held this assessment tool in high regard.

When the results came back, Bob called me to his office. The test results showed I was not a good fit. Bob explained to the test administrators that I was his best salesman. They countered that I was too intelligent for that job, but I was forcing myself to do the job anyway. They argued that I should be in top management. That blew me away— no one had ever said that before!

At work, I was sent to many schools and classes on salesmanship and within four years I was the top salesman at the dealership. As a follow on to the aptitude testing, Grimm's signed up all salesmen for a new Chevrolet program through Wayne State University. It was called "GROWTH". It was an intense two-year program. They sent many, many books, long play records and, of course, tests. The recordings were professors from Wayne State giving lectures on sales psychology and the like.

At the end of two years, I was the only one to finish the program. I received two wood framed diplomas to hang on the wall. I was now officially a *Certified Transportation Counselor*, and, of course, a graduate of the Chevrolet GROWTH program. That program helped me a great deal, and it was a bit of college education that didn't cost me. I still recall one particular book entitled , *The Magic of Thinking Big* by David Swartz. It opened my eyes to possibilities, and again, success followed. At this point, I was selling between 250—300 cars a year. I was having small increases in my yearly income up until then, but upon graduating from that program, my income jumped $10,000 per year. Carolyn and I won many trips from Chevrolet over the course of many years.

I was, in time, promoted to Sales Manager and later to General Sales Manager. I was sent to Detroit to the Chevrolet Academy for two weeks where managers from all over the country were working on all phases of marketing and dealership operations and management.

In 1993 Bob Grimm died and his son and son-in-law took over dealership operations. The both attended a Dealer Twenty group meeting, where the thrust of the session was on dealership profitability. The "professionals" were pushing dealer owners to improve profitability with some new methods. When they returned, these new methods were unveiled to myself and the sales team. I was asked to embrace it and beyond that was also told to enforce it. To me, these new methods were a bit unsavory, and I responded that I could not work with methods I considered borderline unethical. When the owners consulted with the private marketing team hired by Chevy, they were advised to fire me. And that is precisely what they did! This was in 1993, and I was 52 years with a wife, five children, a mortgage and no job.

During this time, I did not have a position of service in the church either. I was merely a *consumer*. But, as I sat in the pew week after week, I prayed that God would make me a worker in His vineyard.

A short time later, a friend of mine at church, Ed Roecker, asked me to join him and some others volunteers at the Peoria County Jail on Sunday Mornings. I declined, saying I thought the prisoners likely deserved to be there. (I had a bad attitude). After he asked me three times, it's as if I heard God say, "If I can't use you there, I can't use you." I relented, and God could finally use me. (I'm painfully reminded that Peter also denied Christ three times. Here I was praying to be used, but when an opportunity arose, I declined!) Thankfully, God is both patient and persistent.

Reflections...

Ultimately saying "yes" to that Prison Ministry opportunity was by far one of the best decisions I ever made. God did use me. If you truly desire to solve spiritual problems — go to where the problems are. God will provide the open door. You must simply step forward in faith and listen to God. He will provide guidance and you will never have to take that step alone.

GOD – EARLY ENCOUNTERS

While having mentioned God's hand in my sojourn up to now, I realize that I must provide some color to the tapestry He was weaving all the while. Over time, I do believe I was being conditioned to be responsive to God's call. But it certainly wasn't a lightning bolt experience. On the contrary, it was gradual with fits and starts. Meaning, most likely, that I gave God fits. But I am convinced that once God begins a good work in the life of an individual, He will see it through to completion.

At an early age, four or five years old, Mom sent me to Sunday school at the Hanna City Methodist Church. My parents didn't go to church. My uncle Earl Isbell was the Sunday school superintendent and rang the bell to call everyone to Sunday worship. My first teacher was a crippled lady named Mildred Schuster. She had the most beautiful smile that I have ever seen. She looked at me, smiled, put her hands on my face and said, "Jesus loves you." This had to be the first time I'd ever heard that familiar expression, and I felt like I was looking at Jesus. Many years later as I studied God's Word, I realized that I wasn't far off in that sense. Colossians 1:27 says,

"Christ in you, the hope of glory". Mrs. Schuster was likely the first person I ever saw His reflection so plainly.

Another teacher in Sunday school named Mrs. Eccles had the same inviting and loving smile. As I got older, I had other Sunday school teachers who had a positive effect on me, as well, including my brother Dick and a man named Dave Thrush. I liked all my teachers and the Pastor, as well. He was a younger man, and although I can't remember his name, I do recall that he related well with us children. He was friendly and always had time for us.

The Methodist church moved pastor's around every few years, but most of them were old. When I think about the early years of my life; I remember that I have always felt a presence of God, an awareness of God and the desire for peace on earth. Perhaps it was because of all the war talk on the news and the hatred that spread so readily. Being born less than a month before the attack on Pearl Harbor, my earliest impressions were of life filled with news of war and conflict.

My Uncle Stobert was a Pentecostal minister and Dad called the lot of them "Holy Rollers. We had little contact with them–but they were always nice to me. They had thirteen kids – but only three were about my age. I had two paper routes as a kid, but they were small circulation numbers providing little opportunity for any substantial income. An older boy had the *Peoria Journal Star* paper route which had hundreds of papers. I carried the *Chicago Daily News* and served only about forty customers. The other paper I had was a magazine called *Gritt.* It came out only once a week. I only had twenty customers for that route. But though my circulation was small, my geographical area was significant. I had to cover the entire town, the good sections and the poor sections. For a small boy, that was a lot of geography to cover. Fortunately, my Dad bought me a new

Sears bike –a red & white J.C. Higgings model. I rode that bike for many years–I did not get another one.

The only tip I ever received was from Uncle Stobert and Aunt Victoria. Once Aunt Vic tipped me five cents. Still, that was quite something as they were indeed "dirt poor". Truth is, the floor inside their home was, in fact, "dirt" – no boards – just the bare ground. They were the poorest ones on my route. Kind of makes that five-cent tip pretty remarkable indeed! My brother Dick told me how the cousins wore old inner tubes over their shoes in the winter because they didn't have boots. The widow's mite comes to mind as they gave – not from their abundance – but from their hearts. Their pockets may not have been full, but their hearts were.

Still, my Dad said most of the so-called Christian folks were hypocrites—the only reason they went to church was to give a good appearance. "They may be good on Sunday, but watch your back the rest of the week," he'd lament.

One of those "good folks" had chickens and Dad bought eggs from him. This gent (named George) would come to our back door and take eggs down to the basement, He'd deposit them on the table, then come up stairs to collect. One time when I was there, Dad said to George, "Let's go down and inspect the eggs before I pay you." When Dad opened the egg carton, there were two eggs missing. George just said, "Oh, you caught me". Dad told him that would be the last time he'd ever do business with him. When George left, dad looked at me and said, "There goes your Christian."

Although Mom and Dad didn't go to church, I can confidently say; Dad was an honest man. I can't think of any time that he was not honorable. My uncle Earl, Dad's brother, told me once that sometimes people would ask him "How can Frank be your brother when you two are so different?" Uncle Earl told them that his brother

Frank had "carried a cup of cold water" for lots of people that they knew nothing about. Dad might not have been a church-goer, but he certainly lived the spirit of Matthew 10:42. "And whoever gives one of these little ones even a cup of cold water because he is a disciple, truly, I say to you, he will by no means lose his reward."

I remember Dad and uncle Earl driving to Bartonville Mental hospital to visit their Aunt Mary Collins. She was their Mother's sister, and sometimes I was invited to ride along. I didn't get to go in, but still enjoyed time with Dad and uncle Earl. After their Aunt Mary died she willed two old houses in Farmington to Dad and Uncle Earl. Both of those old houses needed new roofs. My cousin Roger and I got to go along with Dad and Uncle Earl to help them as they replaced the roofs.

I also remember the time I had a box of candy for an old lady that lived by herself following her husband's passing. He was Joe White who plowed our garden with his team of horses. She lived just down our street, and when I knocked on her door and told her who I was, she called out that she needed help and asked if I would go get my Dad. People knew they could count on him. That stuck with me all my life. But then, I always believed that there were more people who tried to live a clean life. I could tell by their smile and by watching how they lived . My antennae were up, and I was about to be invited to tune into GOD in a big way.

When I was about ten or twelve, my friend Elmer Vogelsang invited me to go with him to their church tent meeting. In the 1940's and '50's, churches would sometimes , in the summer months, put up a tent and have evangelistic meetings for a week with a speaker every night. The Hanna City Presbyterian Church where Elmer and his folks went had such a tent meeting on the grade school grounds. I went with Elmer to see what this was all about. We boys stood in the back by the entrance (perhaps for an easy escape!) I still remember standing there listening to the pastor, Eugene McAllister. At the close of the service, he asked if anyone wanted to ask Jesus into their heart and start a new life? "If you want to do that, just raise your hand," he implored the audience.

Almost to my surprise, my hand went up. I'm not sure if it was conviction, or if I just got caught up in what seemed like the thing to do. I know now that the Holy Spirit was behind all of it and moved me. A lady from their church came out and talked and prayed with me. I even remember her name, Mrs. Doris George.

I felt great. I felt lighter. When I got home and told my parents what happened, they said, "That's fine, now go to bed." I had no follow up and over time I thought, "Maybe it didn't take." I wish it would have. I thought that somehow I would be a different boy and not do bad stuff. Well, a new plant needs tending, and I wasn't tended. So, before long, I was back to wandering in the wilderness. I was left wondering *and* wandering. "What was that?" I questioned. Later in life I realized that God, indeed, was very real in my life, back then just as He is now, and that tent meeting was the beginning of my Salvation.

Reflections

Springboarding considerably ahead in time, after I graduated from Moody Bible Institute, RHMA (Rural Home Missionary Association) sent me to fill the pulpit of a church that needed someone for just that specific Sunday. The first church they sent me to was Hanna City Presbyterian! Talk about Divine intervention! That was a definite God thing!

At the end of my sermon, I told the congregation that I was some fruit they might not know they had planted. I recounted the story of the tent meeting, Rev. McAllister, and Mrs. George who had prayed for me. As my wife and I stood in the receiving line, two older women came to us smiling and one said, as she pointed to the other, this is Mrs. George. She hugged me like a long lost son. That church has invited us back to preach well over one hundred times. Looking back, when Mrs. George came and prayed with me at the tent meeting, I thought she was an old lady, but she probably was in her twenty's or thirty's. I'm so thankful God paved the way for me to thank her in person so many years later.

As I reflect back now upon these early encounters with God, I enjoyed Sunday school; the lessons, the songs we sang, and most of all how the teachers were so friendly and loved us kids. At eighty-two today, I can still remember the names and recall faces of my first Sunday school teachers, my impressions of God, and the church. This is a sobering reminder for any Sunday school teacher to consider the impact a simple smile and acknowledgement of Christ can have on a small child. As Jesus would say, "Go and do likewise".

❧ IT'S TIME! ❧

Getting Right With God

My career was well underway, and Carolyn and I became more aware of our need to "get right with God". I think we both felt something was just a little off or out of alignment spiritually. Initially, I suppose that meant finding a church to attend regularly. I am not suggesting church attendance and getting right with God are synonymous. In fact, they can be mutually exclusive. But this is where and how we began to align with His purposes for our lives.

Her parents' church was all we knew—so we started attending there and within a few months made the commitment to join the church and become Christians. We also became members of the church. The two went together in that culture — to become a Christian meant you had to join the church as a member. Very different for me as all the men sat on one side and the women sat on the other. I could not sit with Carolyn. I found this odd, if not disconcerting. The Apostolic Christian Church was very traditional – and strict – with German roots. Culture ruled the day.

Despite the somewhat significant cultural adjustment, church was actually going well and my brother-in-law, Harold Witzig, soon helped me become a Sunday school teacher. Although I was very limited in my knowledge of the Bible, I enjoyed teaching, and prepared well and tried my best. I learned about other Bible teaching sources beyond the teaching from our pulpit ministers. Specifically, I learned about a Bible teacher named John McArthur. I sent for a taped lesson and was soon digging in to develop a greater understanding of God's Word. Since the pulpit ministry of the AC Church was an extemporaneous reading from a random turn of the Bible's pages, I will simply say it wasn't always the most stimulating or educational. I take nothing away from those faithful lay preachers, but learning and in-depth study were lacking. As was sermon preparation. More often than not, we only heard about repentance. Spiritual growth, sanctification, and spiritual maturity took a back seat to repentance sermons – Sunday after Sunday. That was the predominant repetitive theme from the pulpit. Left to my own devices, I gobbled up many other resources as I became aware of them. Little did I understand that this was frowned upon.

Teaching Sunday School was a seven year commitment and after the seven years of teaching I was back sitting in the pew with my kids, which now numbered three. (We had been married for just four years, but had three kids during that hectic season of life.) I asked Carolyn if she would be willing to be a stay-at-home mother, and forego her nursing career for a time. I promised to work whatever hours necessary to provide enough income for our growing family. She was wonderful and graciously agreed. We both believed our children would be better raised by her than a hired hand.

Within a few years we had two more children. With four girls and one boy the need for money increased and I had to work twelve hours a day and sometimes more than that. A commission-based sales job can be very stressful – sometimes feast or famine. I was so thankful for a faithful and hard working wife. Caring for five children is more than a full time job.

After teaching Sunday School for those seven years, I was later asked to co-teach a class of college students with an older man, Harold Krantz. We met on Wednesday nights in a classroom in the church basement. I don't remember the curriculum but the kids always had questions for us. We took turns teaching, but we were both there to support one another. I remember one night a student asked Harold a question at the end of class. Harold dropped his head then looked over at me. I knew immediately that he did not know the answer (and neither did I, but I proceeded to answer). After the class was over and the students had left the room, Harold looked at me and said, "You didn't know what you were going to say, did you?" I said, "No, but God put words in my mouth." Harold said, "Well, the answer was beautiful."

Reflections

Sometimes, we need to be empty to be filled. That evening with Harold Krantz drove that home to me, and it is a realization that has never left me. Now that I was fully committed to live for the Lord, He finally had me where He wanted me. Or rather, He had me **AS** He wanted me. . . empty and teachable. Where He would lead me from here is remarkable even to me as I reflect on what opportunities He placed before me.

❧ *CALLED TO SERVE* ❧

I do not intend to portray myself as anything but ordinary, and I highlight the following ministries I served not as a testament to me, but to the Lord and Savior who equips those He calls. These varied ministry opportunities are not the resume of a great preacher or even a great servant – but they are testimony to God's faithfulness in using each of us for His purpose and Glory. My path in ministry was not an even road. There were pits and dark seasons. But I do believe they were allowed (or even orchestrated) by God to put me in the right place at His timing. One seminal moment was a dark spot that, in reality, allowed me to truly see His light.

After being terminated from Grimm Chevrolet in July of 1993, I pursued temporary work for two small automobile dealers – just something to keep food on the table and a roof over our heads. I also remained a member of the Apostolic Christian Church, but felt a hunger to more formally advance my Biblical education. I enrolled in a distance learning program through Moody Bible Institute in Chicago. As I mentioned, regrettably, outside formal Biblical education was (if you can believe this) frowned upon by the leadership of the Apostolic Christian Church.

In December of 1994, the Church Elder called me to come to his home. It wasn't a friendly chat, but more like an inquisition. He demanded to know what all I was doing in Prison Ministry. I explained I was helping with the Sunday church service at the Peoria County jail. "What else?" he questioned. I explained that at various times, I would speak at the Peoria Rescue Mission. "Again, he pressed. "What else"? I admitted that I occasionally would be asked to speak at the South Side Misson , and also that I served on its Board of Directors. Still, he pressed. "What else "? I recounted that both Ed Roecker and I also served as Chaplains in the Tazewell County Jail , ministering to prisoners there on Tuesday nights. Back came the now familiar refrain. "What else "?

At this point, it dawned on me what he was pressing for, so I just said it. "I'm enrolled at Moody Bible Institute and am taking several classes. Ah, this was the pivotal point. He nearly came out of his chair and emphatically demanded, "That has got to stop!" He added a not-so-subtle threat, "If you don't cease, I will have to take Church discipline against you." I was flabbergasted. Church discipline, I always thought, was about seeking restoration – not punishment or something to be used as a weapon for compliance. But he had expressed the threat, and that's all I really needed to hear. I knew this would not end well.

The elder further explained his angst. "Don't you know that when you graduate from Moody you will be required to sign that you believe 'once saved, always saved'"?

"Yes," I admitted. "I do realize that, and it's what I believe." However, under his relentless pressure, I caved and did offer that I would stop my Moody pursuits. However, after I got home, I opened my Bible and it opened to Acts 4:19. " But Peter and John answered them, "Whether it is right in the sight of God to listen to you rather than to God, you must judge,... . " Emboldened, I immediately called the Elder back and said I would make it easy for him , and I would just leave the Apostolic Church. He said , "You don't know everything!"

And I'm still puzzled by his reaction. I'll admit, there was much then, and still much today that I need to learn, but I do know the way that the Apostolic Church doled out Biblical discipline is patently wrong.

I've seen it first-hand. Perhaps I should have held my tongue at that point, but I went on to explain that I knew of a family member whose wife was unfaithful. But in the Apostolic Church culture, despite that somewhat common knowledge, nothing was done to his wife. And nothing would be done until and unless she confessed her sin before man. Only then would the church take action. It was definitely a "head in the sand" approach. When I expressed this, the Elder had no comment.

We did relinquish our membership, and I've never been back. I had been a member in good standing for twenty-seven years. This was hard for my wife who was raised in this church, and it was a difficult season. But she agreed to follow me. Her only request was to ask that I be the one to inform her parents. I did just that, and we began attending Grace Evangelical Mennonite Church the very next week.

Following this difficult chapter of my spiritual life, I wasn't sure what God's intentions were. But He knew the next phase of my ministry service about to unfold. I may have been clueless, but God is sovereign. It was happening just as He intended.

Gary Uftring, owner of another large inventory car dealership in Central Illinois had offered me a managerial job , but I turned it down. I just wanted to sell. He accepted my explanation and provided a nice salary, a new car, and a gas credit card. I knew I could make more money as a salesman than as a manager, with the added plus of freedom to come and go as I pleased. And indeed, I did make considerably more money at Uftring's from the end of 1993 to March of 2004 than I ever had before.

But, I came to realize that my focus on money was turning me into a person that I did not want to become. I graduated from Moody Bible Institute in May of 2000 with an Associate's Degree in Biblical Studies. Ironically, it was the same day our daughter Sara graduated with a Bachelor's Degree in Arts.

Three years later, a gentleman came into the dealership asking for me. I learned his name was Jack, and he explained that he was an Elder from Congerville Mennonite church . After we met and greeted one another, I thought perhaps he was looking for a new car. However, he was shopping for something quite different – *and unexpected!* He had read a recent article in the *Peoria Journal Star* about a salesman in Washington who had just graduated from Moody Bible Institute's distance learning program. I had never met him before, nor had I ever attended Congerville's Mennonite Church.

Jack explained that his church was searching for an associate pastor. They were of the same conference as Grace Church in Morton where we were now members. While this encounter was rather a complete surprise to me, I felt as if God placed this opportunity at my feet and asked me, "Will you step away in faith from a large income to serve Me?"

Of course, I listened with a mixture of excitement and anxiety. I told Jack that I needed to talk with my wife before I could give him an answer. He was gracious and understood completely. We parted and I was feeling slightly off balance from this unexpected encounter.

That evening, I drove home immersed in thought and soon after coming into the house, Carolyn and I were discussing God's challenging invitation. We both knew that money would be tight, but concluded that if God wanted us there, it would all work out. This church was only about twenty miles from where we lived, so God certainly had the logistics covered.. I won't say it was an easy decision, but we prayed and talked and talked and prayed and ultimately, both of us agreed. . . we would be heading to Congerville. Shortly thereafter, in a sort of whirlwind process, we found ourselves in a small gathering with the church elders and president of the church conference. The Elders confirmed our decision with the laying on of hands in a prayer, and I was no longer professional sales manager – I was an associate pastor of Congerville Mennonite Church!

I had many duties in that role, but of course one of the first was to visit congregation members in their homes to introduce myself and my wife and to become acquainted. While it ostensibly was for them to get to know me, I also gained a keen insight into where the membership was in terms of their journey with Christ. It was a deep immersion into a whole new experience, and again, I was both excited and anxious. Carolyn and I both felt God's hand, and we knew we not alone.

One of my duties was supervision of the Sunday School programs for both the young kids and adult ministries. I would teach adult Sunday school, and shepherd the establishment of fellowship groups and Bible studies. It was also my job to start the Sunday service with a reading of Scripture and to preach when the Senior pastor was away. I enjoyed the work and especially enjoyed meeting all the people of the church. I had once heard that if you find a perfect church, don't attend because you'll make it imperfect. It's true… the church is a body of believers, but we are all flawed sinners nonetheless. Indeed, I began to note several things about the senior pastor that were troubling to me. But as the new guy, for the moment, I kept them to myself.

It's not my place to judge, but I could sense that the Senior Pastor was paranoid and very much into personal control. In visiting members of the church—many, if not all, had said that the Senior Pastor had never visited them, even the ones that lived very near the church. Perhaps it was just my perception, but he seemed to be generally untrusting of anyone. This made for a somewhat awkward working relationship. We were called to be partners in the shepherding of this congregation, but at times, I felt we were actually at cross purposes. I'm not sure why God called me into such a circumstance, but I put my trust in Him, and strived to be faithful to His calling. Sometimes, there were dark days.

On a personal level, just a year after I assumed my position in March of 2004, I faced another dark season. I was diagnosed with prostate Cancer. I shared the news with the congregation, and asked for their prayers.

Two weeks later I got a call from Senior Pastor Phil and he asked me to attend an Elder Board meeting on the upcoming Wednesday night. When I arrived, I was told by Phil to wait in the dining room until called. Eventually, I was called into the session. There were the three Elders and Pastor Phil in the room. The Elders explained that Pastor Phil had written a bad review of my performance. He reported that I was not helping him, and our collaboration was not working well. They requested my resignation.

One Elder said he had expected me to come into that job "like a house on fire" because I was the top salesman at the Chevrolet dealership. I asked him if he understood that being a pastor and a car salesman were not the same, and I was not the top salesman the first year at that job either. It took me years to grow into that level of performance, and this new role as Associate Pastor was no different. It would likely take time for any new minister to mature into the role. No doubt, I was feeling a bit defensive, but I also felt my argument was valid.

I asked the Senior Pastor if he was the very best he could be during his first year in ministry. He sheepishly admitted that he wasn't. I asked why he would expect or demand that from anyone else. This was met by silence from all. It was clear that they wanted a clean break. They obviously wanted me to walk away without the chance to talk to the church members. I am convinced that deep down, they knew (or at least suspected) that Pastor Phil was shading the truth. But still, he had their backing. The next morning, I cleaned out my office. Sweet Carolyn went along with me, and of course, she wanted to speak to Pastor Phil herself. He was in his office but refused to meet with her and furthermore, would not make eye contact with me. It was so disheartening and discouraging.

Now, I was facing cancer and no job. I maintained health insurance coverage through a Cobra policy, but it cost almost $1000 per month! I elected to have a radical prostatectomy and went to Mayo's in Rochester, Minnesota in April of 2005. After healing I went back to selling cars at the Chevrolet dealership in Washington and remained there until I was eligible to draw Social Security in August of 2008.

To both clear my head and heal emotionally, we took a two week vacation to the Northeastern United States. Friends of ours, Joe and Judy Keen, went with us. Joe had offered, "If you drive, I will pay for the gas." God always provides! We went to Maine, Vermont, New Hampshire, Boston, and Pennsylvania. The three days in Boston and the tour of Fenway Park were highlights for me. God provided a healing respite, both physically, spiritually, and emotionally. And He was still orchestrating how He would next use me as I would soon discover.

Reflections...

I realize now that the dark times came whenever the Lord wanted to move me to another place of growth and ministry. After every dark day or season, the Lord opened my eyes to see with Spirit vision. I have never felt as if God deserted me. I'm sure I may have failed Him often, in some way. I am fully aware that I am a weak sinner, but I also know that He is a Holy God and He meant every experience for my spiritual good.

❧ PRISON MINISTRY ❧

My prior involvement with Prison Ministry began to expand. As I joined other Christians in prison ministry, even from the first Sunday, I was impressed with the love and compassion everyone showed the prisoners. A group of several volunteers conducted services at the Peoria County Jail. We would start at 8:00am and went to 8:45am for the first service. Another group of prisoners would follow and we taught and interacted with them until 9:45am. Finally, female prisoners came for 10:00am services which concluded at 11:00am. Of course, not all prisoners came to church.

If they had been disciplined for bad behavior during the prior week, they would lose the privilege of church attendance. Prisoners in the holding cells did not get the privilege either. Although I did not have an active role in the services, when formal preaching concluded, many individual prisoners approached us to shake hands and to thank us. I told one man that I didn't do anything, and he simply replied, "You came". That uncomplicated, yet profound comment provided considerable food for thought. "We came." What a simple thing to do – yet so often we hold back. We are called to "go forth and teach the gospel". What a privilege to be called to "go". I know I received more than I gave, but that is not uncommon in the service of God. It is indeed, *our* privilege.

The third week that I went to the Peoria County Jail—a man sitting beside me asked if I would like to join him in visiting some other prisoners from his pod that were, for various reasons, unable to attend that day. I didn't know enough to say no, so off we went to K-pod. The guard was willing to buzz us in, but before doing so he asked, "Are you sure you want to go in there? It's been a hot spot of trouble all week." My ministry partner Lloyd said he was sure it would be fine. I was not so sure. But we did continue on. As we went into K-pod, we were met with a semi-circle of individual cells surrounding a game table in the center.

There was a small black and white TV mounted on the wall. It was on and tuned to something – mostly just providing background noise. Five prisoners were playing cards, smoking and glaring at us. Lloyd, announcing our arrival stated that someone had asked for chaplains to visit. One prisoner, a white guy with a black patch over his eye replied, "Yeah, I did." Lloyd asked permission to sit with them and read some Scripture. He also offered to pray with them. They seemed to move in a collective mass in our direction. Lloyd then calmly turned towards me and said, "Go ahead".

I was shocked and shaking (at least internally, if not outwardly). I opened my Bible and read some verses and tried to explain what they meant. When I looked up from my Bible I noticed that they had extinguished their smokes and turned off the television. Soon we were all holding hands while Lloyd led us in prayer! The prisoners asked for Bible Study material. They were hungry for more, and I was touched by how only the Word of God can satisfy such hunger and spiritual longing.

Reflections...

After that brief time together in K-Pod, we rejoined the other ministry volunteers in the gym for the next service. I sat there asking myself what had just happened. I opened my Bible and the first verse I saw was Matthew 4:19. Jesus said, "Follow Me and I will make you fishers of men." I knew precisely at that moment that God promised that if I stepped out in faith, He would do the work. My job was to be His ambassador; His spokesman; His hands and feet. I knew that His Holy Spirit would speak through me. I had but one ability... *availabilty.*

I'll also never forget one day at the female prisoner gathering. A female prisoner stood and proclaimed, "I just want to say to all of you that I came into this prison alone. I will be discharged this coming week. But I am definitely not leaving alone."

YOUTH FARM

I continued in the jail ministry for 15 years. My friend from church, Ed Roecker and I expanded our outreach and began going to the Tazewell County Jail on Tuesday nights, as well. It was about five years into these Jail Ministries that Paul Meister, the head of Peoria County chaplains, asked if I would take over the Youth Farm Ministry. They wanted to have a chaplain come on Sunday mornings and have a church service. Paul said that he was way too busy and wondered if I would take over that ministry. Youth Farm was only a half mile west of the county jail so logistics couldn't be an excuse. I accepted.

Youth Farm is for boys that have been in trouble with the Law or sometimes parents would bring them because they were just more than they could handle. Often, the courts would send some boys there, and still others had simply bounced around the state system until the Farm proved a good fit. Boys ranged in age from nine to seventeen. Youth Farm was part of the Peoria District 150 school system. In addition to academics, students also raised cattle on the grounds, which provided an annual cattle sale that provided the major fundraiser.

The first Sunday at Youth Farm I only had three boys come, so we used a class room. Coming to church was not mandatory. As time went on, attendance grew to twenty-seven boys. We grew into the larger space of the dining hall for church services. I tried to recruit some younger Christians from my church to get involved. I needed help, but most of all I wanted a song leader. I am not a good singer. Some years later, a benefactor left some money to Youth Farm to build their own Chapel. I did get some good volunteer song leaders. A few times a group of Christian teens would come and put on a biblical skit.

As we were transitioning from the dining hall to the chapel, a female worker from the kitchen area approached me and told me how she had to work every Sunday. She would listen to our services, and said, "I hope you don't mind, but this is the only church I have." I felt badly for her. I hadn't realized she was a participant of our church service, and now that opportunity would elude her. I wish I had found a solution for her.

In the new Chapel, I decided to add a Wednesday night Bible Study and the boys were enthusiastic. We got a TV and a video player and I started showing Christian videos featuring missionaries from around the world. I also screened PILGRIM'S PROGRESS. I would first tell them what they were going to see. After the show, I would explain what they saw and how God works around the world.

I tried to vary services from time to time so that the boys could get involved in the service. One example was the Sunday I gave each boy a sheet of paper and a pen and told them to draw a picture of their church. As I walked around looking at their pictures I noticed a Spanish boy by the name of Juan did not draw a building. Instead, he drew a big cross and people sitting on a hillside listening to the chaplain. I asked him to share his picture and explain it to the group. Juan said his church was too poor to have a building, so they sat outside and worshiped. This provided a perfect opportunity to tell the boys that Christ's church is not a building, it is Jesus and His people.

One final memory from Youth Farm was when the Christian music star Carman was scheduled to perform at the Peoria Civic Center. Carman was a popular contemporary Christian singer and songwriter. Youth Farm had been offered free tickets and the boys got wind of that. They pestered me relentlessly to take them to the event. That was a scary proposition. Seven of them wanted to go and I worried how in the world I would be able to keep track of them? I asked my nephew Phil Witzig if he would help me out, because he is a great singer. I thought I had a chance to recruit him, and it worked! Phil went along. As soon as we walked into the Civic Center the boys scattered like dropping a handful of marbles on the floor.

Nothing I could do now but let the show go on and hope for the best. I had never been to a show like that: loud music, flashing lights, and wild colors of clothing. But as the evening went on I could see what Carman was doing. He had to entertain them to earn the right to speak to them. His Message was right on and crystal clear. When the concert ended, the boys found me—I did not have to go looking for them. I had no idea where they had been sitting, but they knew where Phil and I were. Just like God knows where we are – and is earnestly wanting us to find Him.

Reflections...

I once heard someone say there are four paradoxes in life. One must suffer to get well. One must surrender to win. One must die to live. And one must give it away to keep it. All of these, I believe, are Scripturally based. As I reflect on this particular event from my ministry, I am reminded of two truths. The first, that when we empty ourselves, can God fill the void. The second, that human control is an illusion. I gave control of those kids away – whether intentionally or not. But by relinquishing control and trusting them, they returned. I "gave control away, and God allowed me to keep it."

I'm persuaded that every human has a God-shaped hole in his heart. When we yield to Him, He fills it. And then He can use us for His purposes.

ॐ *PULPIT SUPPLY PREACHERS* ॐ

I invested about ten years at Youth Farm, but God had other fields to plow, as well. I soon became affiliated with a ministry known as Pulpit Supply Preachers. This organization is a ministry that helps local churches fill the pulpit in times of need. Their mission is simply to help connect local churches with preachers – from students to teachers to Evangelists – who have a willingness and desire to preach yet occupy no current full time ministry position. It might be for only one Sunday when the resident preacher is unavailable – or it could be for a longer time frame. All I knew, is that I wanted to make myself available. I found a good Christian brother named Greg Menold to take my position at Youth Farm, and I was at the ready. Or so I thought.

The first church assignment was Hanna City Presbyterian, the church where I first encountered those loving teachers. I also got a first taste of this new opportunity while I was yet doing Prison Ministry services. The pastor of a Southern Baptist church in Burlington, Iowa was scheduled to preach at the Peoria County Jail on an upcoming Sunday. The head of our Prison Chaplain group, Paul Meister, asked me to take the Pastor's place in Iowa. Carolyn was unable to go for some reason, so I asked my son-in-law, Trent Sauder to join me, and he brought my oldest grandson, Taylor along, as well. (Taylor was nine years old at the time. He's thirty-five now, and faithfully serving God as a youth leader in his church.)

At the Southern Baptist Church, they had a table in front of the pulpit that said, "Until He comes" As I stood at the pulpit I commented to the congregation that a Mennonite minister stood before them, but I knew we served the same "He" inscribed on the table in front of me. They liked that. On the way home Taylor asked me, "Grandpa, why did the people keep saying "Amen" all the time?" I told him that was their way of saying that they agreed to what I was preaching.

Rural Home Missions in Morton also often sent Carolyn and I to fill the pulpit of various churches — sometimes close by and other times it might be a considerable distance. Churches varied in size from 150 congregants down to as few as seven. Both Carolyn and I enjoyed this ministry opportunity very much, and we met some very interesting and wonderful people.

I started keeping a notebook on where we went and what I spoke about. We were sent to the same churches many times so the notebook became very important.

Two of the churches we were sent to offered me the job of being their full time pastor. The problem was the same with both locations... all the people were elderly – no youth – so not growing. One church had a total membership of seven people and the other had only twelve members. The solution was the same for both; there were good churches within two miles of them that they could go join, but neither of them wanted to do that. I felt that taking either full-time position would only be a short lived solution. Longer term, they needed to merge with other vibrant congregations.

A small church in Plymouth, Illinois was the scene of a rather unique situation. Plymouth is about one-hundred miles from my home. RHMA called me on short notice to fill the pulpit on the upcoming Sunday. I was in the middle of a very busy week, but I said that I could. I didn't have time to prepare a whole new service, so I thought I would just use a sermon from my notebook that I had not used before at Plymouth. Sunday came and I was reading over the Scripture I was intending to speak on. Quite suddenly, I felt a nudge from God that this was NOT the Scripture to use.

As we were driving to Plymouth, Carolyn asked me what I was planning to speak about during services. I sheepishly replied, "I don't know. God just let me know that He wants something different. Don't worry, He will provide."

We arrived soon enough, and as we sat in the front row of the church, Carolyn again glanced at me, and all I could do was shrug my shoulders. "I still don't know," I said. She was likely more near panic than I was. And my calm surprised even me. Following my introduction, as I stepped to the pulpit, it came to me. I knew what passage God wanted. I read the Scripture and walked through the passage as best I could extemporaneously.

Reflections...

Following that service, as Carolyn and I stood at the exit shaking hands with the congregation, two young girls in their late teens or early twenty's approached. One of them was in tears. "That is exactly what we needed to hear today," they said. All I could do was point my finger toward heaven. "It was He, not me," I replied.

❦ HOSPITAL MINISTRY ❦

God then opened a door to continue ministry at Methodist Hospital in Peoria, Illinois. I met all the criteria to be considered for a hospital chaplain's position, and was hired part time. The hours were long – twelve to fourteen hour shifts. And the financial rewards were of no consequence at only $10 an hour. But the opportunity to make a difference in someone's life was beyond worth it. In a hospital setting, one sees people at their most vulnerable moments. One sees heroic care amidst pain, fear, and sadness. But I loved the work and the opportunity to speak and pray with the patients and relatives. But it was not all sweetness and light. Some very challenging experiences awaited me. For privacy reasons I can't talk about specifics. But, with sensitivity to privacy and patient anonymity, I can share insights into this challenging ministry opportunity.

During night shift work, many hours were spent in the Emergency Room. One particular evening a young girl in her early twenties was brought in and was obviously very intoxicated. I was called to her room, and was attempting to visit with her. Not long thereafter, her parents arrived and entered the room.

After a brief greeting and introductions, I advised them what I knew about their little girl's dire situation. I also offered to pray with them, however, the parents and I were ushered from her room while medical staff administered aid to the young woman. Before long, an Emergency Room physician sought me out – informing me that the girl had died. He asked me to go with him to inform the parents. For all of us, it was a life changing moment. If ever those parents needed God's comfort, it was at that time. I still often think of her and her folks. Whatever that young girl was trying to escape from did not work in the earthly sense. Today, all I can add is that she is in the hands of a righteous God.

Perhaps the most shocking episode was the time I was paged about an elderly lady who needed an MRI for a suspected brain bleed. I accompanied her and her daughter to the MRI procedure. As she was assisted to the table and put in position to undergo her scan, she inexplicably lashed out in a man's voice and began cursing and swearing at everyone in her presence. It took five staff members to subdue her. Her eyes glared right and me and laughed loudly. "Hey Priest, come get on top of me!" She again laughed more – an ugly devilish laugh. I was just the chaplain, but it seemed everyone looked to me for what to do next. It was obvious to me that she was demon possessed, and I suggested a sedative. Hospital staff administered the sedative, and she calmed down. She was returned to her room. It was a frightening experience for all, and an unforgettable one, as well. Hospitals deal in the physical realm of body and flesh, but we humans are more than fleshly tissue. Ephesians 6:12 comes to mind... "For we do not wrestle against flesh and blood, but against the rulers, against the authorities, against the cosmic powers over this present darkness, against the spiritual forces of evil in the heavenly places." (ESV)

But there were bright and gratifying moments, as well. Another time I was on the oncology ward one morning, and the lead nurse told me that the man in room 423 (named Larry) was being discharged for home hospice care. When I arrived at the door to his room, a young lady was standing there. She asked if I was a pastor. She explained that Larry was getting dressed to leave, but wanted to get right with God. He didn't have a church home, so I agreed to visit with him. As he finished dressing, we both entered his room. I asked him a simple question. "Why?" I wanted to hear his testimony and statement of faith.

He said he had been a sinner all his life and wanted God to forgive him. That's all I needed to hear. I said, "You pray for forgiveness and I will pray after you." Larry asked, "What do I say?" I explained that he was just going to have a conversation with God, so tell Him what you want to tell Him.

Larry had a very sincere prayer and professed his belief. When he finished, I said, "Larry, you are now a believer and a child of God." God's requirement for the promise of heaven is confession of sin; acknowledgement that we need a savior; and belief in His Son, Jesus as that Savior.

Larry was very grateful, but longed to also be baptized. I told Larry that the thief on the cross didn't have time to be baptized but just the same, Jesus told him that he would be in Paradise that very day. Larry still desired baptism, so we improvised. We put a towel around him, poured water on his head, prayed over him and he was baptized in the name of the Father, the Son, and the Holy Spirit. He was so excited. Two weeks later, I saw Larry's obituary in the local paper. I was confident there was rejoicing in heaven despite the sadness of Larry's passing for his family.

I, too, rejoiced. This was ministry! What higher calling than to lead someone to Christ and his eternal salvation? However, when word got to my supervisor, the joyous celebration stalled. I was reprimanded by the main Chaplain, saying that what I had done was "not my job". It seems everywhere I go God has to bail me out and find me another job. But I will confess, I don't regret my time with Larry – and I'm quite confident as he abides with Jesus in Heaven, he doesn't regret it either!

The final memory I'll share concerns a man named Jim. I had been paged by a Christian nurse in the Cardiac ICU. They just admitted a patient from the Emergency Room that needed immediate heart surgery. When I got to the ward, the nurse signaled Jim's room. I entered and introduced myself. Knowing (as did Jim) that this was a serious medical emergency, I asked him. "How are you with God?"

He replied enthusiastically, "Oh, I am good with God, I pray to Saint Jude every day." Obviously, this prompted me to ask a few more questions. "Do you believe the Bible is God's Word? Do you believe that it is all true and with no errors? Do you mind if I tell you what it says?" I then quoted from John 14:6 where Jesus said, 'I am the way, the truth, and the life, no one comes to the Father except through Me.'"

I told Jim, "You know, St. Jude was undoubtedly a really great man of God, but he is not your savior. All people need a Savior and the only true savior is Jesus." I put my hands on him and prayed. Once again, I was put "on report" for pushing my faith on someone who did not ask for it.

Reflections...

In my younger years, when I was lukewarm towards Christ, I know I gave Him fits. Now, I was on fire for Christ and wanting everyone I met to share in the joy of His salvation. But it seems that while I now was aligned with God, I was at odds with established human authority. How ironic! Hospital leadership wanted me to take three days off to think about what I was doing. I didn't need three days. I volunteered to leave the ministry instead. I served there for four years, and don't regret a day.

ॐ PEORIA RESCUE MISSION ॐ

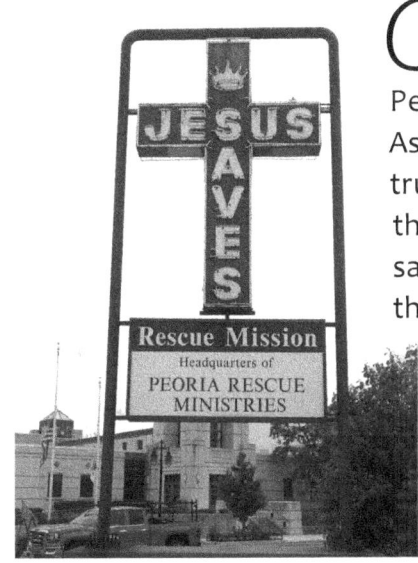

One week later I was at Pine Lakes Golf course in Morton for the Peoria Rescue Mission Golf outing. As I was retrieving my clubs from the truck, Mr. Jerry Trecek, Director of the Rescue Mission walked over to say hello. He also asked, "How are things at the hospital going?" Isn't God's timing amazing? I quipped, "You'll have to ask someone who works there!" He said, "What did you do, say Jesus too many times?" I chuckled, and replied, "Well, Jerry, that is the right question. I believe they are so afraid of being sued that they limit the ministry." Without skipping a beat, Jerry then asked me to come work for the Rescue Mission.

"Doing what?" I asked. Jerry explained that they needed another Christian Counselor. I told Jerry that I had only one class at Moody on counseling. He countered, "But you do have a degree in Bible, don't you?" I nodded. "That's what's most important," he said.

So, just that quickly, one door closed and God opened another. I would soon start work at the Barnabas Center on Knoxville

Avenue in Peoria, right next to the women's pregnancy center, also a Rescue Mission project.

Mike Krippel was the head of the Barnabas Center and a very kind person. Two other counselors: Sheryl Douras and Marsha Zielinski, along with a receptionist, Rosemary Moffitt, comprised the entire staff team. I felt privileged to join this dedicated group, and I was warmly welcomed. Marsha and I shared an office and became good friends. We worked different days, but shared our experiences and our love for books and reading.

Counseling was new to me . We took in clients directly from off the streets. We required each person to fill out a form so we had an idea of their background, any issues, and problems. There were no set fees, just whatever the client could afford. More often than not, this was nothing. We worked with men from the Mission downtown in addition to people coming from the surrounding areas. Some came over fifty miles to the Barnabas Center.

I was tossed into the deep end swiftly. I met with my first two clients almost immediately. Following those sessions, Mike called me into his office to ask how it was going. Each session had been an hour, and I told him for the first 45 minutes, I had no clue what to say. But then, God came, and suddenly, words came freely. Mike laughed and said, "That is how it works. If God doesn't give you anything to say—say nothing." That proved to be very wise counsel.

With now three counselors, if one of us had a troubling session, we would come together, discuss it, and share ideas and approaches. Our work day started at 8:00 a.m. with a time of prayer. First clients would arrive by 9:00 a.m. We took an hour lunch break at noon, followed by afternoon sessions beginning at 1:00pm. We would typically close at 5:00pm, so a normal day would involve counseling two clients in the mornings and four clients in the afternoons when fully booked. Thursdays were the exception—we stayed open till 9:00 p.m. Long days, and sometimes grueling and heart wrenching, but I was one-hundred per cent emotionally and intellectually invested. I wanted to do more in my counseling education.

Mike shared a brochure that highlighted week-long classes in Lafayette, Indiana. These were held every February at Faith Bible Church. I wanted to try it, and the Mission graciously paid my fees. I was fortunate to attend. There were five phases within the learning program, and each had to be taken in order to complete the program. Upon completion, a successful student could then pursue certification as a Certified Biblical Counselor. At that moment, I had no intention of doing that —I just knew that I needed more knowledge in the specialty of Biblical Counseling.

During the program, several PhD's who had actually authored books on Biblical Counseling gave lectures by the hour from 8:00 am until 7:00pm with a lunch break mid-day. Students had awesome access to these authors, and had opportunities to talk informally with them during breaks and between classes. I was hooked.

I returned to Lafayette five times and completed all the classes. But once again, it was not a trouble free path. There was a dark season to travel through, and it not only caused me to defer my certification, but also challenged me as never before.

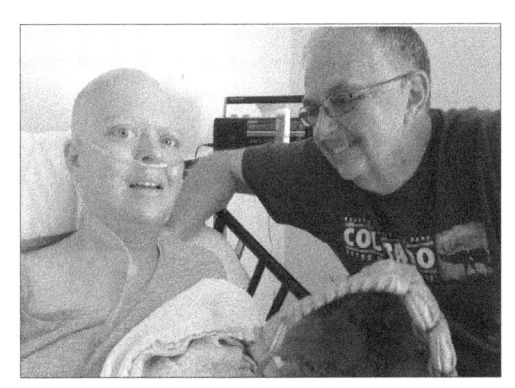

At the beginning of 2015, our youngest daughter Sara had a huge lump appear under her left arm. Our family doctor authorized a surgical referral, and a surgeon removed it, but no biopsy was performed. Later that Spring, in April of 2015, Sara was being treated for a severe and persistent cold, which would not get better. She was sent to OSF Hospital in Peoria for a chest x-ray that revealed something suspicious. A follow up MRI was performed and highlighted a large tumor compressing her lungs. A biopsy confirmed cancer. Standard protocols of both radiation therapy and chemo were prescribed, but no treatment proved effective. Treatment was initially performed locally in Peoria, but through the generosity of friends, Sara also was seen at MD Anderson Cancer Center in Houston. The advanced stage of the disease process unfortunately meant nothing could be done for her. As a last resort, OSF offered an option for a radical chemo protocol.

Sara considered that option to continue, with the prospect of maybe having another sixty days of life – or she could cease treatments, in which case her life expectancy was a mere thirty days. Sara pondered this briefly, and calmly said, "Take me home." We brought her to our home on hospice care. Sara's end of life journey transpired rapidly. She was diagnosed on her birthday, April 30th, 2015, and passed into glory on September 26th, less than five months later. During this painful season, I obviously stopped working on my Counseling certification. I didn't pick it back up until six months after Sara passed.

Despite this dark and painful process that she and we endured, Sara was an inspiration. She had the best attitude; displaying a wonderful sense of humor and wit. We were supported by our church and many friends and extended family. But there were many sad times to process through. I fondly recall when our music pastor dropped by with his guitar; sat on the floor in Sara's room; and played and sang whatever song she wanted to hear. Her visitation and funeral were at Grace Church. One of the funeral directors approached me late during her visitation and commented, "Jim, you'll need to get more friends because our count tonight just surpassed one thousand!"

This season was no easy passage to wade through, but by the grace of God, Carolyn and I saw through it to the other side. Grief was still there, but we also knew Sara was at peace and in God's presence in the arms of Jesus. We were ready to rejoin the world of the living.

So, I again picked up my certification process for Biblical Counseling. To complete the process, I had to answer twenty-three questions on Theology and an additional twenty-three questions on Biblical Counseling. After my papers were submitted in type-written form, they were graded by my assigned supervisor in Dallas, Texas . I passed! The next phase of pre-certification was to perform sixty hours of supervised counseling. I was assigned a counseling supervisor in North Carolina. Remote supervision was accomplished by recording client counseling sessions (with their approval, of course). Each session was submitted to my supervisor for review. I'm thankful for the rigor, and while challenging, this was the journey that God led me on.

Every counselor seems to gravitate to a specific aspect of counseling with which they are more comfortable. Mine seemed to be Marriage Counseling, and those issues that involved anxiety and depression.

Were all the sessions successful? I could only wish that were true. A sage piece of advice Mike provided went something like this… "If we, as the counselor, are working harder than the client – that's a problem." We all had our share of those problem encounters.

In the sphere of marriage counseling, it was all too common for one partner to desire it but the other partner clearly opposed. I can't count the number of times a couple would come in with a mantra such as, "You have to change him." Or "No! You have to change her!" It was important to level set expectations, so my reply would always be the same. " I can't change anyone, but I can introduce you to someone who can. His name is Jesus."

The sessions would then evolve into my questioning both parties. "Now, each of you tell me where you think the problem starts." Most of the time that would slow down the accusations hurled at one another. For a Biblical Counselor, the only tool in the toolbox is the Bible. And of course, that was my most often advised reading resource. Often, however, I would provide them a copy of *Purpose Driven Life* by Pastor Rick Warren. I would show them the book and read the very first sentence from "Day One" (Pastor Warren didn't use chapter numbers, but rather categorized each section into "Days" – Day 1 through Day 40.)

But Day one, sentence one always set the tone: "It is not about you!" And that one sentence can aid us all. If we want to understand the purpose of our life — we must simply start with that realization. Jesus said basically the same thing in Matthew 22:37-40. "[37]And he said to him, "You shall love the Lord your God with all your heart and with all your soul and with all your mind. [38] This is the great and first commandment. [39] And a second is like it: You shall love your neighbor as yourself. [40] On these two commandments depend all the Law and the Prophets."

Pastor Warren had created a pithy summary sentence, but the sentiment is the same. There is a God, and it's not you! Put Him first. It really isn't all about you!

Frequently, I would also query the couple by asking "Do you each want your marriage to be healed?" If they affirmed that basic tenet of counseling, then I would ask if they would follow my instructions completely. If again they confirmed that they would, I would offer this specific advice…

'Sit down at the table, not a sofa or a place where you could fall asleep. I recommend the kitchen table, as we all anticipate something good when we sit at that table. Next, read Day One from Warren's book out loud. Discuss it. Ask each other, "What did it say? What does it mean? What do we need to do differently in light of what it said? After your discussion I want you to hold hands and take turns praying for each other. Now, repeat this process every day for all forty days of the book. Each day is only about three pages, so it is very doable."

In my experience, when a couple faithfully followed this advice, did the assignments, and engaged prayerfully with one another, I would more often than not hear something to the effect of "Man! This is so powerful!"

In Scripture, 1 John 4:10 puts it this way, "In this is love, not that we loved God but that He loved us and sent His Son to be the propitiation for our sins. Beloved, if God so loved us, we also ought to love one another." This is Matthew 22:37-40 in action. This is the life we are called to. It's not about "me", but it is about God and others. When we get out of our own way, God can (and does) work in our hearts in powerful ways.

The sad truth, however, is that it takes both partners. If both of them are not fully committed, nothing will work. There is simply too much self in the way! Jesus gave up His rights for us, we need to give up self for Him. I put up a white board in my office to draw diagrams on. Some people need more than words – they need to see what the words look like. But whether audibly or pictorially, the message is powerful. Die to self, and you can truly begin to live the life God desires for you.

There are many evils in our world to draw us away from Christ. One particularly pervasive temptation that many men struggle with is pornography. There are many verses in the Bible regarding sexual impurity. I counseled many men in this regard.

I would start with Matthew 5:28, which is part of the sermon on the Mount.. Matthew 5:27-28, "You have heard that it was said to those of old, You shall not commit adultery. But I say to you that whoever looks at a woman to lust for her has already committed adultery with her in his heart."

Then I would turn to 2 Samuel 11:2-5 to relate the story of King David's temptation and fall. "Then it happened one evening that David arose from his bed and walked on the roof of the King's house. And from the roof he saw a woman bathing , and the woman was very beautiful to behold. So, David sent and inquired about the woman. And someone said, Is this not Bathsheba, the daughter of Eliam, the wife of Uriah the Hittite? David sent messengers, and took her; and she came to him, and he lay with her, for she was cleansed from her impurity; and she returned home. And the woman conceived; so, she sent and told David, and said, "I am with child."

And lastly, I would turn to 1 Corinthians 6:15-20. *"[15] Do you not know that your bodies are members of Christ? Shall I then take the members of Christ and make them members of a prostitute? Never! [16] Or do you not know that he who is joined to a prostitute becomes one body with her? For, as it is written, "The two will become one flesh." [17] But he who is joined to the Lord becomes one spirit with him. [18] Flee from sexual immorality. Every other sin a person commits is outside the body, but the sexually immoral person sins against his own body. [19] Or do you not know that your body is a temple of the Holy Spirit within you, whom you have from God? You are not your own, [20] for you were bought with a price. So glorify God in your body."*

Reflections...

Even when we think we are done — we are not done! Or perhaps more appropriately, God is not finished with us! God provided a wonderful open door for me with Biblical Counseling.

Every thought, every action we take will bring a reward or a consequence. No exception. We cannot blame our circumstances. Circumstances do not make the decisions for the actions we take. We are each responsible for the things we do. In the case of King David — what he did ultimately led to the death of Uriah, Bathsheba's husband. Sin is not innocent fun where no one gets hurt. There are always consequences of hurt and the sin cannot be undone. But praise God! It can be forgiven.

While no woman ever came for counseling about porn, that does not mean it is not an issue for the female of the species. The sins of this world are common to all—and all sin eventually leads to anxiety and depression—sooner or later. And if left unrepentant, it leads to death.

This is why I love Biblical Counseling—God's answers bring results without pills to numb the body or mind.

I retired from the Rescue Mission at the age of seventy-eight. But Carolyn and I still work for the Lord by helping with the "Grief share" program at Grace Church in Morton, Illinois. I also still teach adult Sunday School one quarter of the year and teach a Bible Study in our home on Wednesday evenings. Still, God is not through with me. With us. And I'm so grateful!

PERHAPS, ONE FINAL MINISTRY

Scripture tells us in Ecclesiastes that "there is nothing new under the sun", and at the age of seventy-eight, most of us might believe we have seen it all. But even at that seasoned stage of life, God held another as yet unveiled surprise opportunity and chose this moment to lay it at my feet. It was one I was most unprepared for; was shocked by; and questioned with incredulity.

I am registered as a Certified Biblical Counselor on a familiar business website known as *Linked In.* This business networking site is familiar to many professionals and boasts that it is *"the world's largest professional network with more than one-billion members in more than two hundred countries and territories worldwide."*

While in my home office one day, I received a *LinkedIn* message from a Vice President of CitiBank in California. His name was John Owen. His message suggested that we needed to talk. His message further claimed that he had recently discovered that I was his biological father! I called my wife into my office and said, "Look at this! I wonder what kind of a scam this could be? Somebody looking for money, no doubt." I had been happily and faithfully married for over fifty years , and being this man's father was simply not possible.

After some hesitation, I finally typed a reply that we did NOT need to talk. .

It wasn't long after that our daughter Joan, who was living in Ft. Collins, Colorado called. She asked Carolyn, "Mom, what is Aunt Geri's son's name? Is it John Owen?" Carolyn handed me the phone. Joan asked me the same question, and I replied, "No, my nephew in California was Todd Jones."

Joan explained that a Mr. John Owen had called her with a shocking revelation. It seems that previously, Joan had submitted her DNA profile to Ancestery.com. This John Owen had done the same. Through this seemingly benign and random effort of both Joan and John, , they discovered that John and Joan were a sibling match!

John had related his story to Joan, and she shared it with me. John had been adopted as a baby in California. He detailed that he had enjoyed a great life. His adoptive father was the head of the Apollo Space program and his adoptive mother ran multiple real estate offices in California. They were wealthy, and his life was good—but now, both of his adoptive parents had passed of cancer, and John was on a quest to find his biological parents.

Through his research, he found his mother in California, and connected with her. As they chatted, he naturally sought to identify his biological father. She had to admit she did not know who it was. It was then that he then sent his DNA to Ancestery.com and learned of the Isbell DNA connection to Joan. Further investigation revealed the larger Isbell clan in Central Illinois. He obtained Joan's number and called her. She, in turn, called us.

After John talked to Joan—he told her that he was afraid to call me – both because of my initial reaction to his *LinkedIn* message, but moreover because he read my *LinkedIn* biography and noted that I was listed as both a pastor and a Certified Biblical Counselor. John told Joan he was *definitely NOT* a religious person. Undeterred, Joan encouraged him to call me, claiming that "Dad was a good guy and It would be all right."

After hearing this incredible story, I knew I needed to make this right. I looked up John's phone number from his previous attempted contact, took a deep breath, and called him. My first words were, "John, I may owe you an apology, but first, may I hear your story?"

He began with the same disclaimer he had professed to Joan. "Look, he said, "I am not at all religious." I said, "That's great! I'm not religious either." John was taken aback. "I don't understand," he said. "But aren't you a pastor and a Biblical Counselor!" "John," I tried to explain tenderly, "I am. But religious people are not good—they are the ones who had Jesus killed."

John relayed the details of his research… when he was born, where, and his mother's maiden name. Realization hit me. I remembered dating this woman when I got out of the Navy, and that she had subsequently moved to California. I never heard from her again. After a long chat, when all the facts were on the table, there was no dispute. I indeed had a son named John Owen that I previously knew nothing about.

We talked for a long while. John told me all about his life. He had been married and had a daughter. He bought her a house in his neighborhood. She was married and had three children. Then he told me that his wife had left him and later he married a man. He was gay. His adoptive parents told him when he left for Cal State that he should stay away from three things… drugs, alcohol, and religion. They told him that he could recover from two of them, but not from religion. As a result, John's knowledge of the Bible was significantly limited although he is quite a brilliant man. He was honestly just seeking to answer one of life's great questions... "Where did I come from?" From these seeds, I hoped to likewise help John grasp the bigger question, "Why am I here?" I eagerly anticipate the day I can tell him that he is here to glorify God. I know God is patiently waiting.

Reflections

We have been out to see John twice. He is a most gracious host. He and his partner have also visited us here in Illinois once. We have enjoyed great conversations and I can sense God working just by the questions he and his partner have asked. I am attempting to guide, counsel, and shepherd as God allows.

All of our children love John, and accept him and his partner as family. But we will not shy away from opportunities to share God's Word. We will not judge, criticize, nor condemn. We will, as God commands, love John. And we will share the Word, and pray for his sojourn and full acceptance of God's truth.

Drawing upon the experiences God has provided throughout my lifetime – including both the dark seasons and seasons of joy, I will not squander this surprising opportunity to once again minister His truth. I am so grateful.

John is my long lost son. He is someone I care about as God's creation. He, too, was created for a purpose to glorify God. I pray that God will allow me to sow Gospel seeds, and I will trust Him to provide the increase.

Final Reflections

*I*t is impossible to record all of life's memories. Some are forgotten, of course, and some for the sake of brevity are omitted. But one ministry I cannot fail to mention. The most important ministry I've had is that of spiritual head of our household. Specifically, being father to our five children – Becky, Joan, Andy, Jackie, and Sara. The blessings and privilege of that call to serve should not go unacknowledged.

With gratitude and humility, I proclaim that these five children have been a source of tremendous joy, fatherly pride, and untold blessing. With their own children now numbering fifteen, and at present seven great grandchildren with four more on the way – I can't begin to recount the richness of their impact on my life's tapestry. This ministry was a door God opened with the birth our first daughter, and He has never closed it. It is a continual ministry that I am supremely challenged by, yet humbly grateful for. And I must include my newly discovered son, John, as well. I know God created him for a special purpose, and I'm grateful He has placed him back into my life at this point in time. Truly, I'm reminded of Psalm 127: 3 "Behold, children are a heritage from the LORD, the fruit of the womb a reward." (ESV) Truly, God continues to bless us abundantly, and His rewards are sweet. Other ministries I've served have been but for a season. This most important ministry has not been time limited – it has been for a lifetime and continues to this day.

I suppose all other ministries I've served have one curious constant. They've all been marked by frequent starts and stops I've experienced along the way. Doors opened – then closed. Opportunities stripped away, and new ones prepared in their place. I can see now in every case, when God moved me – even when it was a painful episode – He opened yet another door of ministry on the other side. When my wife and I reflect, and even look ahead, only one thing has been and will remain constant. "God is good all the time, and all the time God is good."

I remember as a child that Hanna City had lots of stray dogs—I believe that people who didn't want their dogs anymore would dump them off in Hanna City. As a result, there were many homeless dogs scrounging for food. My Mom would put leftovers outside the back door to feed those homeless dogs. My Dad didn't like the dogs hanging around the back door and tried to chase them away by shouting at them and sometimes hurling firecrackers at them. But, Mom kept feeding them—and they kept coming back!

That's an apt illustration in the biblical sense for our ministries. Whether to aid people addicted to drugs, alcohol, pornography, to break a bad habit, or simply get right with God. We need to show people that what shows up on the "back porch", is what we keep feeding. Sin is a hungry dog – and never satisfied. When we stop feeding it, it retreats – seeking other "back porches" to feast upon.

Christ came to take that hungry dog away. Through His death, we are freed from the penalty of Sin. We are justified. Through His Holy Spirit, we are being sanctified from one degree to another – and are thereby freed from the power of sin. When we die and join Him in Heaven, we will finally be freed from the presence of sin. No more hungry dogs. It is a wonderful promise. And I believe it. Do you?

Finally, as I reflect upon the entirety of my life, I am irresistibly drawn to 1 Timothy 1:12–17:

[12] I thank him who has given me strength, Christ Jesus our Lord, because he judged me faithful, appointing me to his service, [13] though formerly I was a blasphemer, persecutor, and insolent opponent. But I received mercy because I had acted ignorantly in unbelief, [14] and the grace of our Lord overflowed for me with the faith and love that are in Christ Jesus. [15] The saying is trustworthy and deserving of full acceptance, that Christ Jesus came into the world to save sinners, of whom I am the foremost. [16] But I received mercy for this reason, that in me, as the foremost, Jesus Christ might display his perfect patience as an example to those who were to believe in him for eternal life. [17] To the King of the ages, immortal, invisible, the only God, be honor and glory forever and ever. Amen. (ESV)

APPENDIX

Left to Right: Becky, John, me, Carolyn, Andy, Jackie, and Joan"

Blessed beyond measure!

Jim & Carolyn